WITNESSING NURTURING PROTESTING

Therapeutic responses to sexual abuse
of people with learning disabilities

by
ALAN CORBETT
TAMSIN COTTIS
STEPHEN MORRIS

introduction by
VALERIE SINASON

illustrations by
GEOFF JONES

David Fulton Publishers
London

David Fulton Publishers Ltd
2 Barbon Close, London WC1N 3JX

First published in Great Britain by
David Fulton Publishers 1996

Note: The right of Alan Corbett, Tamsin Cottis and Stephen Morris to be
identified as the authors of this work has been asserted by them in accordance
with the Copyright, Designs and Patents Act 1988.

British Library Cataloguing in Publication Data

A catalogue record for this book is available from the British Library

ISBN 1-85346-338-8

Typeset by The Harrington Consultancy, London
Printed in Great Britain by BPC Books & Journals Ltd. Exeter

Contents

Acknowledgements

Many people have contributed to the development of Respond and to the thinking expressed in this text. Our sincere appreciation and heartfelt thanks go to: Valerie Sinason, Dora Rickford, Haldora Blair, Rosemary Morris, Lady Katya Lester, Ian Mitchell, John Walker, Gregor MacAdam, Gloria Wade, Richard Davis, Dr Ann Craft, Janet Hughes, Emerald Davis, Chris Cherry, Nerys Hughes, Malcolm Brown, Alain Rias, Joel Xharrd, Dr Heather Allen, Bernie Lassinger, Dr Earl Hopper, Geoff Jones, Christiana Horrocks, Professor Sheila Hollins, Peter McKeown, Pam Cooke, John Southgate, Kate White, Brett Khar, Judy Davis, Ailish Doyle, Graham Getgood, Annabel Poate, Stephen Mendoza, John Henry, DI Greg Barry, Jenny and Paul Taylor, DI, Maggie Goodwin, Jo David, Margaret Robson, Lydia Sinclair, Dr Shaun Gravestock, Annie Moser, Elizabeth Pothig, David Simpson, Janis Stanford, Hilary Brown, Alix Brown, Margaret Kennedy, Wendy Keelan, Helena Kennedy QC and David Blunkett MP.

Special thanks go to all our clients. Grateful acknowledgement is given to the Department of Health and to all those who contribute to the funding and financial security of our work.

Glossary

Within this book terminology is used which may vary according to the different settings in which it is used. We hope this glossary will help provide clarification on our meaning. It is to this end that it is provided, rather than an attempt to outline prescriptive definitions.

Advocate: Therapist supporting client through recovery from trauma. Defined by Alice Miller (1983) as 'a trustworthy, sincere support figure, not complicated by theories.' Roles of advocate as originally outlined by John Southgate (1991) fall into four parts – witness, protester, nurturer and translator.

Client: Person being seen for psychotherapy. May also apply to person being worked with by other professionals, such as social workers, psychologists, etc.

Conscious: The part of a person's mental activity which deals with the immediate.

Counter-transference: The state of mind in which other people's feelings are experienced as one's own.

Depression: Condition in which the client suffers from low spirits, difficulties in assimilating thoughts and actions and delusional self-reproaches. Often viewed psychoanalytically as a pathological form of mourning.

Disclosure: The process in which a victim begins to communicate to another how they were abused.

Free Association: Mode of thinking in the client encouraged by the therapist to communicate thoughts without reservation or inhibition. Will often lead to communications from the unconscious.

Learning Disability: Commonly defined as being in place if a person's IQ level falls below 70, and has impaired social functioning. Broadly defined under Mild, Moderate and Severe, depending on levels of IQ. Respond moves the emphasis away from cognitive abilities to an awareness of the impact of trauma on functioning ability.

Mourning: Reaction to loss, whether loss of a loved one through bereavement, or the complex set of losses incurred by being sexually abused.

Nurturer: In being a Nurturer, the Advocate acts to addressing the low self-esteem engendered by trauma suffered by the victim.

Post-Traumatic Stress Disorder: Set of extreme reactions to abuse, including recurrent and intrusive recollections of abuse, recurrent dreams related to the abuse, sense of reliving the abuse, distress at exposure to events which evoke the abuse. Other symptoms include sleep disturbances, persistent increased arousal, irritability, anger, aggression, hypervigilence and physiological reactions to events resembling the abuse.

Psyche: The mind.

Psychiatrist: A medical practitioner concerned with clients whose presenting symptoms are concerned with the mind. Unlike psychotherapy, medically trained psychiatrists may make use of medication in work with clients.

Psychologist: Person trained in any form of psychology, i.e. the study of behaviours and systems of thought.

Psychotherapist or Counsellor: Provider of regular, clinically supervised sessions with client. Should be in a recognised training or have completed a recognised training. Should be member of a recognised training body.

Psychotherapy: Broadly defined as any form of 'talking cure' – although the work of Respond recognises the validity of non-verbal communications within the therapeutic relationship. Should be regular, clinically supervised, and able to incorporate work on the unconscious, transferences and counter-transferences.

Protester: In being a protester, the Advocates acts to voice anger at the injustice of the trauma suffered by the victim.

Sexual Abuse: Threatened or actual sexual exploitation of another.

Survivor: Person who is within therapy or who has attained emotional distance from his or her sexual abuse.

Transference: The process in which the client experiences the therapist as though the therapist were another figure from the client's life.

Translator: In being a translator, the Advocate acts to interpret verbal and non-verbal communications of the effects of trauma in ways which the victim can readily comprehend.

Trauma: Any unexpected experience which a person is unable to assimilate.

Unconscious: The part of a person's mental activity which deals with processes of which the person is not actively aware. Memories of abuse are often to be found hiding in the unconscious, and only come out in the form of dreams, free associations, etc.

Victim: Person who is still in trauma following their abuse, either chronologically, emotionally or both.

Witness: In being a witness, the Advocate acts to confirm the reality of the trauma suffered by the victim.

Introduction

In Belgium, on the way to the first international conference on psychoanalytic thinking and learning disability, June 1996 organised by Dr Johan de Groef, I found myself struggling with limited French in order to find the right ticket and platform for a further train journey. A rather miraculous machine, that spoke in several languages, answered my difficulties. Without such a machine and without the kindness and linguistic knowledge of strangers, my experience would have been very different. Had I been traumatised – a refugee, for example – the event would have been even worse.

What is life like for the learning disabled men and women in this country for whom ordinary aspects of life like shopping and travelling are transformed into 'foreign' experiences for lack of verbal language? On one of the single bus-driver/bus conductor buses I witnessed a painful scene when a young learning disabled man, holding up a long queue by fumbling in his pocket for money, eventually offered a five pound note for a 50p fare. The tired and irritable driver pointed to the 'Correct fare only' sign, shouting 'Can't you read, stupid?' The humiliated young man snatched his money back, swore, smashed his fist on the plastic window and ran off. What would it have taken to transform that situation?

Whilst holding that situation in mind, imagine now a conference on sexual abuse and its consequences in adult life. Imagine it as an ambitious one with parallel sessions as well as plenary events. BUT imagine it as a conference planned with and for learning disabled adults such as the young man trying to get on the bus. Imagine the care that goes into providing visual maps describing where to go and what the subject is. Imagine the planning required to have professionals available as verbal information centres to provide information on times and rooms for those unable to read. Imagine, in other words, a context in which the inherent emotional intelligence of the learning disabled human being is acknowledged and the environment actively seeks to provide whatever is needed to inform that individual's mind so that choices can be made, followed and enjoyed.

Once you consider the beauty and ambitiousness of such a concept of true normalisation you have the heart of 'Respond' who not only regularly organise such conferences but whose philosophy coherently shines through all their administration, treatment, design, pamphlets, therapy rooms and waiting room.

Imagine an ideal waiting room for adults who have experienced severe distress in their lives. What kind of temperature, light, furniture or design would be facilitating? What would the therapy rooms be like? What kind of aesthetic style would be facilitating?

Most of us have experienced waits in hospitals, clinics either for ourselves or someone close. We are aware of the way the actual objective reality of the external environment impinges in our mental state or relieves it. How an organisation deals with the physical surroundings that contain human distress is important. Where individuals have been sexually abused, have had the environment of their body and its furniture disarranged and soiled, the message the external environment gives by its provision is significant. The increase of 'rape suites' in police work, comfortably furnished rooms in which rape victims can struggle to recount their painful experiences, bears testimony to the inter-connection between inner and outer worlds.

'Respond' is a unique counselling and psychotherapy service for learning disabled men and women who have been sexually abused (and for some, who as a result of past experiences, have also become abusers). Its comfortable waiting room with *free* coffee, water and tea machines is an external sign of the internal care it provides for its clientele. Its house style is of disturbing and moving black and white paintings by Geoff Jones that do not minimise their emotional power but convey it with disturbing simplicity. Their rooms have boxes of tissues, comfortable seating and lighting, simple stones, ornaments.

I have known and admired Steve Morris, Tamsin Cottis and Al Corbett separately for over a decade. Active in the self-advocacy movement and determined to create as much autonomy as they could for their clients, they also sought additional advanced professional and personal development in mainstream psychodynamic thinking. In other words, they have been part of that small but influential group of thinkers in this field who have always wanted to integrate the best aspects of each discipline for the purpose of providing the optimum environment for their clients. I deeply admire their commitment to learning disabled men and women who have been sexually abused and their determination to provide something of excellence.

In 1991, whilst there were pockets of concern regarding abuse and disability, notably from Ann Craft of Nottingham University and Napsac, Hilary Brown and Vicky Turk at the University of Canterbury, Professor Sheila Hollins at St George's Hospital Medical School, Margaret Kennedy of Keep Deaf Children Safe, Julie Boniface of Voice (now chaired by Edwina Currie MP) and myself, then primarily at the Tavistock Clinic (and currently setting up a disability service at the Anna

Freud Centre and working at St George's Hospital Medical School), there was no central treatment centre. Indeed, sexual abuse was considered something that did not reach the handicapped.

There were no national guidelines on procedures for vulnerable adults and there was no critical mass of popular opinion that could support the concept that these vulnerable children and adults could be further hurt. Unable to communicate well, unheard, deprived of sexual education and privacy, the tragic symptoms of abuse were retranslated into proof of handicap. 'He masturbates all the time as an infantile gratification'. 'She needs a self-care programme as she mutilates her vagina'. 'He strips off all the time in public because he has no sense of social skills'. The madness of the abusive acts was mirrored by the professional madness of the social and legal response. The fact that severely learning disabled adults are still largely not seen as viable court witnesses aided the exclusion from the normal protective safeguards of society this particularly vulnerable group.

When Steve Morris and Tamsin Cottis decided to set up a treatment centre there was no built-in funding or peppercorn offered premises. There were also no permanent staff (see Chapter 2). There was also a prevailing political and social pressure to 'hush up things' in the services. Through listening to the painful testimonies of their clients they were determined to change this. In addition to their prior qualifications (in social work and counselling) they added on further training and supervision to underline their motivation to aid their clients to their uttermost. In five years RESPOND has deserved its continued reputation as a key treatment centre.

This book is not only an important outline of the way Respond developed, although that is helpful for other individuals who might be inspired to put their own hopes into practice. It also provides an account of the theories that have proven valuable in practice (Chapter 3) and takes the reader through the process of Disclosure (Chapter 4), Core issues that follow disclosure (Chapter 5), the relevance of attachment and loss (Chapter 6), case examples (with details carefully disguised to ensure confidentiality) (Chapter 7), group work with women (Chapter 8) and professional issues (Chapter 9).

In dealing with men and women who have faced multiple abandonment in their lives, the centrality of broken attachments and malignant abusive attachments echoes throughout the book. Not surprisingly the work of John Bowlby, Alice Miller and John Southgate (of the Centre for Attachment Based Psychoanalytic Psychotherapy) are central here. RESPOND have delineated four advocate roles that inform their work, the advocate witness, protester, nurturer and translator and I find these compatible with the psychoanalytic role of acting as an 'auxiliary ego' (Sinason, 1993) for the learning disabled patient. A key aspect of all these advocate functions is the willingness to hear and accept the patient's testimony.

Respond, like all of us working with sexual abuse, are painfully aware of the secondary damaging effects of disbelief and denial in the therapists and counsellors. Comments such as (Chapter 4) 'It's in the past', 'Do you really expect me to believe that', 'you were too little for it to have any effect' silence and corrode the soul of the victim.

The learning disabled victim is double damaged by abuse. The low self-esteem that follows abuse often pre-exists in these clients, due to their internalisation of hostile wishes towards them from the family and the wider society. Without a cognitive process to speed up the healing process, it is possible that such victims are more vulnerable to repetitions either through passing on the abuse directly or by being sexually exploited .

The existence of RESPOND offers hope for the abuse victim and the abuse victim in the offender. It offers the rigour and responsibility of treatment and concern.

This book is a clear and moving distillation and crystallisation of all Respond have learned and pioneered up to this moment. They generously offer their learning experiences and recommendations to shorten other peoples' journeys. The seamlessness of the writing styles echoes the excellent clinical and administrative teamwork of the authors/clinicians.

As with all creative people, they do not rest on their solid achievements. New projects are already in the air and with them the embryos of new books. Look out for them!

CHAPTER 1

Development of Respond

Five years ago, when the idea for Respond was first conceived, we had no base, no permanent staff and no funding at all. The drive behind the idea was the testimony of the adults with learning disabilities that we were seeing through our work in Adult Education and the voluntary sector.

The account of Respond and its work is by necessity quite personal at times. It is not possible to be so concerned with the issue of sexual abuse without there being considerable personal consequences, both positive and negative. We are presenting this book about working with people with learning disabilities who have been sexually abused in a format which also describes the development of a structure within which the work can take place. We didn't begin with a blueprint, or a set of guidelines about developing a service and nobody told us what to do, although lots of people have supported us as we've done it.

In 1991, Stephen Morris and Tamsin Cottis were working independently of one another in London with adults with learning disabilities. Both had been inspired by the development of the Self-Advocacy movement. We shared its beliefs that people with learning disabilities should have control over their own lives and should have as much personal autonomy as possible. We knew that those working with people with learning disabilities should have the attainment of such autonomy for their clients as the central focus of their work. We recognised that fulfilling the aims of self-advocacy was a difficult process and developing all the time. Our working experiences had demonstrated that we needed to be creative and flexible in listening to people and not prescriptive about what form empowerment was going to take in the lives of the individuals we knew and worked with.

Both of us recognised that the area of personal relationships was a central part of this process of empowerment. If you take a couple of moments to reflect on the most significant events in your life so far – when you've been happiest, saddest, your greatest hopes for the future – these will probably be connected to the significant relationships in your life. Of course we agreed then that much needed to be done in the way that services concerned with housing, education, work and health for people with learning disabilities were provided. Not enough of these were organised in a way which put the wishes of the client first but were instead directed by resource considerations and a reluctance on the part of professionals to relinquish their power to clients.

What was clear in 1991 and remains true today is that there is an emotional agenda as well as a political one. By this we mean that if there truly was a revolution in the way that services were provided and people with learning disabilities could, for example, live where and with whom they wanted; have meaningful and purposeful things to do during the day; have more money and more control over that money, we would still not have achieved everything. There is no guarantee that people with learning disabilities would then achieve positions in our communities where they were valued and respected as citizens of equal worth to those who are not disabled. One reason that this would be the case is that we have not paid enough attention to the emotional needs of people with learning disabilities. Providers of services should recognise that learning disability is often accompanied by psychological trauma; that people with learning disabilities are often lonely and isolated; that their early experiences have often contributed to this situation and that because of it they are extremely vulnerable to abuse. Perhaps more than any other issue, sexual abuse highlights the meeting place of the cultural, political and emotional damage inflicted on people with learning disabilities. This has been powerfully described by Professor Dick Sobsey in his *Integrated Ecological Model of Abuse* (Sobsey, 1994).

We can see this clearly when we consider exactly why people with learning disabilities are so vulnerable to sexual abuse. Research from the University of Kent suggests that there will be at least 1,000 new cases each year of sexual abuse perpetrated against people with learning disabilities (Brown and Turk, 1993).

In 1991 this research had just begun, and like all of those concerned with sexual abuse we were basing our views not on what had been empirically established but on what we had experienced through our direct work with clients – on what they had told us and on what we had seen for ourselves.

Five years ago, we knew that people with learning disabilities were vulnerable to sexual abuse on a number of levels. During a discussion in a sex education class for women, Susan, a woman in her forties who had spent 20 years in a long-stay hospital told me that she had been raped by other patients in the hospital and she told me that there was nothing anybody could do about it, because, 'It happened all the time'. I can still access the shock I felt when I heard what she said and her comments illustrate painfully and vividly the way in which sexual abuse can become such an integral part of the life of an institution that rape, which most people would consider to be a most traumatic and shattering event (and one which is recognised by the criminal justice system as such, carrying as it does, the possibility of a sentence of life imprisonment), was an everyday experience for Susan and one with no possibility of redress. Susan was vulnerable because she lived in an institution with a culture of abuse. She was also vulnerable because she lacked the confidence and the self-esteem to speak out about what was happening to her. No one cared enough about her to make it stop and she knew that was the case so she didn't tell anyone. What messages had Susan received about herself throughout her life which meant she didn't think it would matter to anyone else that she was regularly raped? When the 5-year-old daughter of a friend of mine was sexually harassed at school by a little boy of the same age, she told her mother straight away and straight away her mother informed her teacher. Although neither were able to make false promises about stopping the boy, or others, from doing the same kind of thing, the daughter could know that she didn't have to be treated badly and that someone, or some people would take her seriously when she spoke out about it.

Susan maybe knew better than to make trouble because the hospital was her whole life and if she did something to upset the people who were in charge of it then they may well treat her badly. One thing we realised at the start and know even more about now, is the way that people are punished for making other people uncomfortable when they raise the issue of sexual abuse. So often it is the messenger who is 'shot' and not the perpetrator. This would surely have been the case for Susan. In a large institutional setting, passivity can be a virtue prized above all others. Susan had quickly learned to be good and quiet and accepting of her treatment. And when we look at how people with learning disabilities who do challenge services are treated, we should not be surprised by this passivity. If you have learning disabilities, the expression of negative emotions may be a thing which others feel they have a right to control through medication or through physical restraint or through modification of your behaviour. Only in more recent years, with the development of Gentle Teaching and more sensitive provision for disturbed clients, has this begun to change. Many of the people who come to Respond and those we were working with 5 years ago had no such opportunities and have grown up under pressure to be happy and grateful.

Susan had the words to describe what had happened to her, many others do not. Indeed, the Kent research indicates that 70% of the learning disabled victims in their study had additional communication difficulties. The very fact that learning disabilities are often accompanied by communication difficulties means we should be extra vigilant in listening out for things which would be difficult for anyone to express. Once again, communication which takes the form of difficult behaviour is too often taken at face value, and repressed or redirected without a search for its root cause. In the setting that I met her, Susan was receiving her first ever 'sex education'. Many of the adults we work with have not had access to long-term effective sex education which will teach a sexual vocabulary, the importance of sexual boundaries and of the right to say no to bad touch.

If Susan had made complaints about what was happening to her, it is unlikely that the legal justice system would have found any room for them. As a person with a learning disability, it is unlikely that any court would have considered her to be a reliable witness so she might never have had the chance to give testimony at all. As her attackers in this case also had learning disabilities, it is hard to believe that any police force operating at the time would have been willing to proceed with any action and it would have been left to the hospital to deal with the matter. Imagine if you were a social worker, raped by another social worker and for this reason alone the police refused to get involved. In the past 5 years there has been a growing number of voices raised in protest at the injustices of the legal system, in cases where there is a sexual crime and a vulnerable witness. The work of VOICE has been significant and in March 1995 the Law Commission published a report on mental incapacity. Change is slow, but the need for it is increasingly widely recognised.

People with learning disabilities are vulnerable to abuse from those who are paid to care for them. Mary was another student in this class and she had lived with her family and then moved into a house in the community. Each evening she received obscene telephone calls from her support worker. Jane was followed home and raped by a member of staff from her day centre, Anne was forced by the headteacher at her school to have oral sex with him. David was abused within and then recruited by a paedophile ring which centred its activities on a football league of teams from day centres for people with learning disabilities.

People with learning disabilities are poorly protected from those who have set out to target them for abuse precisely because they are so vulnerable. Since we started Respond, a great deal of work has gone into devising structures which will protect people with learning disabilities from abuse within services, not least is that done by NAPSAC (ARC and NAPSAC, 1993). There are many people who are suffering the long-term consequences of not having been protected and still many loopholes through which determined offenders can slip.

Susan was estranged from her family, but we have known from the beginning that people with learning disabilities are vulnerable to sexual abuse within the family, too. In this they are like children without learning disabilities. They are different in that they may stay at home for much longer. Although we would have been reluctant to believe it in 1991, we know from our work at Respond that people with learning disabilities can be abused because their parents are so angry that they are disabled. Joan was sexually abused by her stepfather who hit her as he raped her and shouted at her that he was doing it because she was 'stupid and ugly'.

We are more conscious than ever of how people with learning disabilities are vulnerable to sexual abuse. We recognise that there is a growing willingness within society to recognise that abuse of all vulnerable people does happen and hope that this will have the effect of making life safer for people with learning disabilities. It is very important to keep this vulnerability in our sights at all levels of service provision.

When we first began to plan Respond our foremost concern was the lack of support available to victims of sexual abuse. There were very few places where a person with learning disabilities who had been sexually abused could receive counselling or recognition of the trauma he or she had suffered. Our feeling at the beginning was that sexual abuse was perceived as a problem for staff and services and efforts to hush things up and protect colleagues led to an abandonment of the victim. Rose was told not to tell anyone after a male member of staff had lured her to his flat and tried to take her clothes off. He was suspended from work and she was believed but still the staff felt they maintained some ownership of what Rose had experienced. We wanted Respond to counter this tendency – to provide a space where the victim's voice would be heard and respected and to make space for the individual responses to abuse. At that time, it was difficult to understand that the victim may express feelings of love for his or her abuser, or of regret that circumstances following the abuse had meant that they were now apart. We didn't know then about the power of attachment. But we did respect our first clients when they expressed these apparently incredible sentiments.

We also knew when we started that there were a lot of workers in the field of learning disability who felt strongly about the sexual abuse of their clients and wanted to be able to address the issue. They told us they felt disempowered to do so that they lacked the necessary expertise to support their clients with such traumatic events and memories and that often their management refused to confront what was going on or had gone on in the lives of their clients. Within 3 months of announcing in the professional press that we were anxious to hear from others concerned about sexual abuse and learning disability, we had heard from over 300 people. At first we had thought a list of places to get support would be the most useful thing we could do. After a few weeks we realised that any list compiled at that time would be very short, as there were so few sources of support, and that perhaps it was a direct service that was most urgently required. At this point we were encouraged by our contact with people with learning disabilities who had been abused and by those who cared for them. We had 20 years combined experience of work in the learning disability field, but neither of us felt qualified to work intensively with the issue of sexual abuse. In the 5 years that have elapsed since then we have acquired a great deal more experience and training. The work has taught us many new things and at times we have struggled to keep pace with the material we have been presented with. Respond has been driven by the combination of our increasing capacity to hear the most terrible things, and what our clients are telling us. In this way, our roots in advocacy and empowerment are still intact. We have learned that the nature of sexual abuse and its consequences for victims will have significant effects on the way a service concerned with these issues will be provided. For the remainder of this chapter, I will consider what it is we have heard and how that has affected the way that Respond has developed. Because we started as an organisation with no funding other than that which we could generate ourselves it has not always been a smooth journey and we would be deluding ourselves to say that pragmatic considerations have not played a role. But we hope to make it clear that our essential concerns have remained the same – to provide a service which supports people with learning disabilities who have been sexually abused and to support those who work with them.

Initially, we saw our clients in the context of other work – myself with groups and clients seen on a private basis and Stephen through his provision of counselling at the service he was then director of. This work had begun as work concerned with sexuality and relationships. It seemed that when people were given recognition of a sexual life and identity it had the effect of granting permission to speak out about bad sexual things which had happened to them. As someone on a course said recently, 'We started thinking it was about giving people sexual rights so they could say, "Yes" but now we realise it may be more about the right to say, "No".' Concurrently with this work we developed training courses for workers and found that there were large numbers of staff desiring more information and the opportunity to consider how they, in the context of their work situations would be able to support people who had been abused.

On our training course, participants begin by thinking about how sexual abuse work makes the worker feel and acknowledge this emotional response as key to what happens next for the client. Sexual abuse puts people in touch with many painful feelings, sometimes based on their own experiences of sexual abuse. If you have a capacity to empathise with your clients then getting in touch with things which cause them pain will cause you pain too. All through the work there is a balance between recognising the pain and separating from it in order to be able to help. In the early days we were aware of this and would still maintain that the best work is done when you really care about your client. What we didn't fully realise then – as we asked participants on courses to share the many ways they got support and sustenance including, for example, using aromatherapy oils, or talking things over with friends – was the crucial need for structured and expert supervision in this work if one is to avoid the pitfalls of denial; over-identification with the victim; of feeling that some things are just too horrible to think about; of experiencing profound effects in one's personal life.

As Respond has developed we have become more sure that it is not possible to exclude the emotional power of the work. Indeed, we have taken care care to keep the emotional agenda a priority in every aspect of our understanding of sexual abuse.

We spent some time seeking a definition of sexual abuse which encompassed what had been experienced by the people we were working with. Much of what was already written applied to children, and some to adults without learning disabilities. We needed to find a definition which could embrace the issue of consent, as well as describing the emotional impact of a physical act. We assert that sexual abuse involves an abuse of power and a betrayal of trust. There has to have been a lack of consent but we recognise the important work that Turk and Brown have done (1993) in identifying that there may be meaningful barriers to consent, put in place by a relationship which has an imbalance of power at its core. A number of our clients who have been abused by members of staff, for example, have consented in as much as they placed themselves in a position where they knew abuse was going to take place. Indeed, Tina – who was abused over many months by a day-centre worker who visited her and sexually abused her in her own home – talked powerfully of her love for this man and her sorrow that someone else's disclosure had led to his dismissal and the end of what she felt was a love affair: 'I didn't like what he made me do, but I loved him'. What he had done was force her to undress and shower and have sexual intercourse with him, after which he penetrated her with objects. The worker abused his position of power over Tina in a sexual way.

We recognised from an early stage that our working definition of abuse would not be limited in terms of the sexual activity it described. Rachel was verbally incited by staff in the hospital where she lived, to perform a strip-tease during 'Top of the Pops'. There was no physical contact in this sexual abuse. Other clients told us of acts of sexual violence; of oral, anal and vaginal penetration. We know that long-term consequences of abuse are predicated by the relationship which exists between abused and abuser, as well as what acts took place, over what period of time and with what degree of fear and coercion.

The emotional power of this work must be recognised and harnessed. People with learning disabilities are dependent on those that care for them in many ways. We have sought to work in a way that ensures that the emotional agenda of our clients is not dictated by what we as workers are prepared to work with. A case was referred to Respond in which a young female victim of sexual assault had initially been denied treatment because her keyworker, who had herself been sexually abused in the past, felt that that the way to get over it was to 'just get on with your life and try and forget about it'. The worker has a right to deal with her own past in this way, but not to prescribe this for her clients.

There is a range of emotion which may be evoked in you as a worker when you are dealing with sexual abuse. You may feel guilty – that these terrible things did not happen to you instead, or that you are unable to make them not have happened. You may also feel guilt that you are in some way making things worse by being the person who assists in the process of bringing up painful memories which distress the client. You may feel shock, horror and disgust at what you hear, and rightly so because sexual abuse is shocking and horrible and disgusting. You will need to ensure that these feelings do not transfer so powerfully to the client that they are silenced by them. There may be times when you feel overwhelmed and burnt out because you have heard so much. It is our experience at Respond that to receive adequate support for these feelings can be enormously strengthening. This support does not judge you as weak for being affected in this way. Sometimes, when people are describing in detail what has happened to them, you may feel sexually aroused yourself and then feel guilty because of this. Honestly recognised, these feelings can provide you with insight into the complexity of the abusive circumstances as experienced by the client. Often you will experience strong anger – at the injustice at the heart of every abuse. This anger, if not contained, could overwhelm the client, although in its right place it can be a powerful motor for action.

Everyone engaged in therapeutic work with clients at Respond has their own weekly, personal therapy and all attend a supervision group. In addition, many attend individual supervision concerning their caseload. This is accepted practice in psychotherapy. What we have had to do is recognise that good supervision is essential in all abuse-related work and we advocate for this very strongly in all our dealings with workers.

Through doing this work we have found out that victims of sexual abuse are men as well as women and that perpetrators are women as well as men. Our clients are aged from 14 to 60 and come from a variety of racial backgrounds. We have learned not to assume anything in terms of who is capable of doing what to whom. If we start with a view of abuse which presupposes, for example, that women will abuse only when a man is telling them to, or that ritual abuse does not exist, we will be doing a disservice to our clients whose abuse experiences contradict our assumptions. We will not be able to hear what they tell us. When we started, we found it hard to accept that people with learning disabilities could themselves be sexual abusers. Indeed we didn't really think about the abusers very much at all, preferring to split them off from the picture, safe in our knowledge that they were 'bad' and the 'victim' was 'good'. We began with a very positive view of our client group and had spent many years speaking up on their behalf. To accept that there is an offending side to our clients (and to ourselves as well) has been extremely challenging. But it has been necessary if we are demonstrate to our clients that we can bear to go into the darkest places of their minds with them. We can do this and still hold on to the pain of their experiences as victims of abuse, and still work with them in a spirit of respect for their humanity.

We have recently begun to gather information about our clients' backgrounds and experiences more systematically. Initially, we did not want to know very much about who came to us in order that our minds would remain clear to work with what they presented us. We still want to be able to do this but recognise that we must examine how and in what ways our service is successful for those who use it. We also want to further our understanding of sexual abuse and learning disability. What early experiences pertain in the lives of victims and offenders? Who will go on from being a victim to being an offender and who won't? How can we work with people who don't use words? A large part of our work is to respond to consequences of abuse but we also want to understand what causes it to happen and to have a clear picture of the context in which it takes place.

How a victim of abuse is responded to when they 'tell their story' or disclose will profoundly affect how much more they are able to tell and how soon they will begin to recover. Disclosure is not a finite thing. The first mention that 'my Dad touched me' may be just the prelude. Our clients will test the water first, see if they will be believed and respected before going on to tell more. There must be a framework for responding to disclosure. Every organisation needs a written statement of how it will proceed so that staff can feel confident in taking disclosures seriously. At Respond we began with the view that each individual had a right for their disclosure of abuse to be kept secret if that was what they wished. This belief was born of our commitment to users rights and it has not withstood the test of time. People with learning disabilities are more vulnerable than other people and we cannot deny their dependence on service providers. It is not professionally responsible to decide that a person can remain in danger. What we continue to do is to try to take the client with us if we are going to have to tell someone else, and to stay there for them in all that follows. Tom told us that his stepfather was physically abusing him. He didn't at first want us to tell anybody because he was terrified that he (Tom) would be made to go and live somewhere else. We told Tom that he was strong and right to tell us. We worked closely with his social worker, explaining how Tom felt and insisting that he act quickly. The social worker intervened and Tom has not had to leave – though this may happen. It is not our role to decide that Tom is better off with his family and getting hit, just because the alternative is a painful separation. Instead, we must work with the social worker and with Tom, addressing the complexity and pain of the situation. We must live with the fact that there may be no satisfactory solution and know that even if there isn't, we must still be there for Tom.

In this respect we cannot offer confidentiality in the way that a mainstream psychotherapy service can and we cannot promise to abide by the wishes of our clients. However, we will not work to a prescribed agenda in our therapeutic service and will work only with what the client brings to sessions. We will feed back to referrers as to whether a client is engaging in sessions and if a referrer has concerns about the therapy we will answer these in a way which does not reveal the content of sessions. We make our conditions of working clear at the outset, emphasising that a person will need support in their therapy, that they will need to be brought to it regularly and on time and that the content of sessions will only be shared in very particular circumstances. In this we attempt to put the client first at the same time as acting responsibly, and whilst also being sensitive to the concerns of referrers who also have a crucial role to play in recovery.

These issues are ones which we at Respond have had to address but they are relevant for anyone working in this field. You may well meet resistance from others who feel that you are raking over the past unnecessarily and in a way which is distressing to the client. You may be called upon to talk about the work you are doing in a way which compromises the confidentiality you wish to offer the client and you will very likely have to make difficult decisions concerning the disclosure of painful information, in the knowledge that it will be hard to achieve a positive outcome. Sexual abuse is nearly always shrouded in secrecy and this is a source of much pain and terror. It is often easier to deny what you know. If you are sharing things with colleagues and not working in isolation it will be harder for you to hide in denial. Organisations must set up systems to ensure that information is shared and that there is a common response to disclosures .

One of the biggest challenges which we have had to face is about the approach we will take in therapeutic terms. It is increasingly commonly accepted that counselling following traumatic events is beneficial and we certainly accepted this as fact when we began working. In the time since we have been providing direct work with clients, we have had to think very hard about what we actually do in sessions. A lot of our core beliefs are set out in subsequent chapters, but it is worth noting at this point that we did not have these set out for us when we started. Indeed, psychotherapy and counselling for people with learning disabilities is still very much a new field. Valerie Sinason has done a great deal to win wider recognition of it and has been a continuing source of support to us. The books which tell you how to do it and which approaches will be successful are simply not there. At the beginning we were aware already of the powerful effects which occurred just by providing somebody with a space to talk about what they wanted to. This space would not be interrupted, it would have firm time boundaries and it would be private. The job of the listener was to be valuing of the client and non-judgemental. The listener would not share their own experiences or seek to offer solutions or tell the client what to do. All the time that we have been doing this work we have been hungry for more information and ideas that would illuminate our practice. In the advocate roles, in identifying core issues, in the work of Alice Miller and in Attachment Theory we have found much which has been helpful. Increasingly, we are working in ways in which we look at what is underneath what people are saying, no matter how unpleasant this may be. This journey is one where the client leads although the more we can bear to see, the more he or she will reveal. We did not anticipate that this would be the depth of the work when we started. At all times we have been learning from our clients.

Although sexual abuse is a painful and emotive subject, which will inevitably touch you personally if you decide to address it in your work, it actually becomes more manageable and possible to contain if professional structures are sought within which to work with it. The horror of a person's abuse can be held in our minds if we can see that the resulting trauma may be about loss. If we can see that core emotional consequences of abuse such as guilt and fear will be causing difficult behaviour, and if we recognise that good support systems for ourselves will give us the strength to go on offering support.

If all of us, at whatever level, can acknowledge and respect that our own feelings will play a large part in our response to any incident and channel those feelings productively, be they of shock, horror, disgust, fear, anger, frustration or guilt then we need not be overwhelmed by the feelings, or waste time and energy in trying to keep them buried as it is damaging to our clients.

CHAPTER 2

The Advocate Roles

When someone with a learning disability has been sexually abused those involved in their daily care are faced with an immense challenge. This challenge was clearly articulated by a residential social worker who, having heard one of her female clients disclose experiences of sexual abuse, asked 'How can I be there for her?' This important question indicates the expressed wish unconsciously communicated by the survivor when they first speak out about their experience of sexual abuse. It is a wish for belief and recognition and for holding and containment. The expressed need in the unconscious wish is for a safe and non-abusive attachment. The residential worker's question in this case indicates the answer. The most important requirement for the survivor of sexual abuse is that the desires of their unconscious wishes are met and that they are not further abused by being abandoned. 'Being there' for the survivor should not be underestimated.

Living with the secret of undisclosed sexual abuse results in a unique sense of loneliness and isolation often experienced as rejection and abandonment. The experience of abandonment is a constant theme recognised and articulated by those attending counselling and psychotherapy sessions at Respond. Listening with care to their experiences it is possible to recognise that prior to the trauma of sexual abuse there is always an earlier experience of abandonment. There is a core experience of abandonment related to the fact that our clients have been born with a learning disability and the consequent realisation of the experiences of that difference are experienced psychically at birth and later consciously throughout life – resulting time and time again in experiences of rejection and abandonment.

Before we can consider how to 'be there' with the learning disabled survivor of sexual abuse it is important to recognise abandonment as the link between the experience of being sexually abused and the experience of having a learning disability. A young man entering the consulting room for the first time said, 'There are two horrible things in my life, my sexual abuse and my learning difficulty – what one are you going to do something about?' This young man was brave enough to name the two awful things in his life and shocked me into realising that for me to be there for him then I needed to recognise both his experiences and then work with both. Whilst I was working with this young man I was also co-therapist to a psychotherapy group for men with learning disabilities. In both contexts the issue of abandonment was a painful reality. In the group the men talked openly about a variety of issues in their lives. It was not until the final month of the group, however, that the issue of learning disability itself was ever mentioned by any of the men or indeed by ourselves. Following a particularly painful session when several of the men had talked openly about being sexually abused one of the men said 'I think it happened to him because he's mental, that's why I get spat at on the bus every night, people say "oh look they're all mental from that day centre", that's why they spit at us'. Again this man was making the link between being abused and having a learning difficulty. Others have spoken about their own awareness of not being wanted, talking about 'coming out wrong' 'not being a real baby' 'being born mad' and 'parents who wanted to send me back': all revealing how the basic right to exist for our clients is brought into question by many in our society.

It is difficult to imagine the loneliness and isolation such experiences of difference bring about. There are many relational aspects of working in the field of personal services. If these relationships are to offer meaning then there is a need to ensure that we address these experiences of abandonment. Recovery and healing from sexual abuse can only occur when the underlaying experiences of abandonment are recognised and not repeated.

The core beliefs (Southgate, 1989) of our clinical practice were inspired by the work of John Southgate of the Centre for Attachment Based Psychoanalytic Psychotherapy in London, the work of Alice Miller (Miller, 1992) and John Bowlby (Bowlby, 1969). These combined influences provide an effective model of advocacy. The 'Advocate Roles' (Southgate, 1989) has provided us with a way of being there for the abandoned learning disabled survivor of sexual abuse. The model enables us to be there whatever our role or discipline. It is certainly not dependent on a clinical setting or indeed on professional qualifications. The concept of an advocate and advocacy will be immediately familiar to those involved with services for people with learning difficulties. The terms are usually associated with the support of someone to obtain basic rights and to ensure that their voice is heard. It is an effective way of addressing powerlessness and providing people with opportunities that they would find difficult to obtain by themselves. Here we are using the terms in the context of the healing and recovery process following experiences of sexual trauma. In terms of empowerment the aims are, however, not dissimilar.

Alice Miller provides a useful definition for the role of an advocate when she describes an advocate as 'a trustworthy, sincere support figure, not complicated by theories'. Miller's definition (Miller, 1983) provides the important message that to be there for the survivor need not be complex, the advocate model is simple yet powerfully effective. It enables those without specialist training to fulfil important roles that provide the survivor with the longed-for recognition, containment and safety all crucial in ensuring that the healing process extends beyond the specialist setting and becomes integrated into the survivor's daily living environment. Recovery from sexual abuse extends to all areas of an individual's conscious and unconscious life. The healing process should therefore not be confined or limited. All staff providing relational services have both a responsibility and opportunity to practise and fulfil the role of an advocate.

John Southgate also illustrates the simple nature of effective therapeutic advocacy when he states what an advocate is not (Southgate, 1989). The advocate for the survival process is not a substitute parent, not even a benevolent one and certainly not the idealised parent that the survivor may never have had. The advocate is not an educator, guru or wise instructor or benevolent conditioner. The advocate is not a blank screen to project upon. The advocate is not an impersonal expert or scientist and is not an example of enlightenment, authenticity, spiritual purity, self-actualisation, or a living representative of some pure quality – e.g. Marxism, feminism – which the survivor is morally pushed to imitate. The advocate is also not the possessor of some esoteric or scientific knowledge whose dissemination will cure clients. Southgate, in stating what the advocate is not, is inviting us to be confident in being ourselves when assuming the role of advocate. It is an invitation to relax and to trust in our ability to be with someone, offering trust, sincerity and support.

There are four advocate roles that facilitate the healing and recovery process: the advocate witness, the advocate protester, the advocate nurturer and the advocate translator. Essential to all these roles is the ability to engage in communication with the survivor and to be aware of all communication both explicit and implicit, verbal and non-verbal, conscious and unconscious. Above all what the advocate witness is required to do is to listen and to be with the person requiring support, giving undivided attention. This may appear simplistic, and although this is true in one sense, people in our culture rarely give or receive such attention. Listening provides recognition and is the most effective intervention in providing a solution to address past experiences of abandonment.

The Advocate Witness

The role of advocate witness provides for the survivor both practical and emotional experiences of being recognised. The advocate witness is able to see, hear and believe what others cannot. As Valerie Sinason points out 'if seeing and hearing means seeing and hearing terrible things then it is easier not to see or hear' (Sinason, 1992). This is not only applicable to survivors of abuse who cannot bear the pain of their own experience, but to others who in recognising the awfulness of abuse cannot bear to think it is true. It is not unusual for survivors of abuse to tell about their experiences only to be met with disbelief. Disbelief as a defence against having to think the unthinkable can have a devastating effect. There is seldom a witness to incidents of sexual abuse and with no one to confirm what the survivor knows to be true the very sense of self and reality can be eroded. The presence of an advocate witness prevents further denial and enables the survivor to identify and recognise what has been done. The advocate witness is not blinded by perceptual rules and is able to see beyond what appears to be socially acceptable. Workers who are able to 'blow the whistle' and report professionals of abusing provide an example of how the advocate witness is sometimes required to cross powerful boundaries and barriers. The advocate witness is brave and strong enough to look at horrible things and to name them as such. The advocate witness assists the survivor in facing the truth, who has done what and how. Witnessing the pain of abusive experiences is not easy but unless the reality is acknowledged then the survivor remains alone with it. Anything other than recognition is denial.

In practice the advocate witness may also be required to recognise other issues that may or may not be directly associated with the reported incident of sexual abuse. Examples of this could include: changes in daily routine to avoid times of vulnerability, consulting with other staff and professionals to help them witness what has occurred and being there for the survivor through any investigation or legal process. All are practical expressions of the advocate's ability to see, hear and give recognition.

The Advocate Protester

The main role of the advocate protester is to reverse the belief that to protest against abusive regimes is wrong. The advocate protester enables the protesting voice often silenced in childhood (Miller, 1992) to be heard again. Many of the people we see at Respond have been effectively silenced for many years not only by the sadistic threats of those who have directly sexually abused them, but also by carers, parents and professionals who have responded to even mild protests with silencing punishments. People with learning disabilities who speak out against injustices committed against them are often deemed trouble-makers and when they are driven to protest further can find themselves controlled by medication or harsh regimes. Gill, who was being sexually abused by a care worker, explained in therapy that she had given up telling people what was happening to her because when she told other staff she had been stopped from watching television. Sally was 20 when she explained that her father had been abusing her since she was 7 and because he was a teacher and served on a local council committee no one had believed her. This young woman was able to have her protest taken seriously only when she started to self-harm.

The advocate protester won't say 'honour thy father and mother' 'spare the rod and spoil the child' or 'that children should be seen and not heard'. The advocate protester will work to free the silenced voice of protest and give the protest the respect and recognition which is rightly deserved. When someone who has been abused is silenced in their attempt to protest about it the consequences can be devastating. Alice Miller in *For Your Own Good* (1987) makes clear that the natural reaction to abuse is anger. If this anger is not recognised or allowed then the abused person is compelled to suppress it and to suppresses all their feelings and memory of the experienced trauma. Later they will have no memory of what was done to them (Messler-Davies and Frawley, 1994). Exposure to such a process of denial can lead to impaired mental health and secondary handicap (Sinason, 1992). The presence of an advocate protester is essential to good mental health.

The advocate protester may be the only voice to say that a crime has been committed, that wrong has been done, that it was not the fault of the survivor and that the abuse should never have happened. The advocate protester can get angry on the survivor's behalf, encourage the appropriate expression of anger, contain overwhelming rage and encourage communication so that anger can be communicated and released. Enabling the appropriate expression of anger provides the survivor with an opportunity for justice. They may not have their voice heard within a legal process or by the courts but the therapeutic effect of a silenced voice being heard should not be underestimated and is certainly an experience of justice.

The Advocate Nurturer

One of the most striking features of many survivors of sexual abuse when they first present for treatment is the diminished state of their self-esteem. Again, low self-esteem in the learning disabled survivor of sexual abuse is related to both having a learning disability and to having been a victim of sexual abuse. One young man described the condition of his low self-esteem explaining that 'I am a no person, no one recognises me, no one knows me and no one see's me'. He continued 'sometimes I think that I am not real, that everything that has happened to me is a dream – where am I?' His searching question was also asking 'who am I?' and is a painful reminder that if we cannot feel good about ourselves then our very sense of self, our relationship to others, the world and our core identity is at risk. The young man who was brave enough to ask those questions could only do so when there was an advocate who was able to witness him and to protest at his plight. He also required the warm and caring intervention of an advocate who was able to be nurturing.

The advocate nurturer is an essential role in addressing low self-esteem and its consequences. The advocate nurturer is able to create a safe, warm and accepting environment. Many people with learning disabilities have not only endured complex institutional regimes of abuse but have also contended with harsh and punishing environments. Many residential settings bear no resemblance of a home, with the physical surroundings having a distinct lack of comfort and care. The advocate nurturer will often be required to address such issues. Making a room warm and comfortable can give the much-needed message that 'you are worth something' that 'you deserve nurturing and comfort'. If the advocate nurturer can take time to give attention to the setting in which the person lives or where they meet to talk together then the task to increase a positive sense of self-esteem will begin to be addressed before anything is said.

Establishing a safe environment should also consider the ongoing personal safety of the survivor. In the current framework of community care it should be possible to ensure that the victimiser is removed from a residential unit, day care centre, school, college or work setting. Sadly this does not always happen. No victim of sexual abuse should be expected to co-exist with the person responsible for the crime against them. The advocate nurturer should be prepared to ensure that this is not allowed to happen.

The advocate nurturer has a crucial role to play in ensuring a sense of safety to the survivor. This is essential if the survivor is to progress to full recovery. Unless the survivor feels safe they will be unable to move through the painful process of healing. One of the consequences of sexual trauma is the loss of power and control. These losses are experienced internally in relation to the survivor's own body, emotions and thinking and externally in relation to other people. The advocate nurturer must be able to address each of these areas, although this may appear to be an overwhelming task it is important to recognise that no one can establish a sense of safety alone. The fact that the survivor can experience the advocate as offering a new relational experience that is safe and secure is the starting point. It is often the first time that they have experienced being close to someone in a non-abusive way. Offering a safe relationship will provide an important new experience that provides a secure base from which the survivor can proceed with their recovery process and eventually enjoy the benefits of other safe relationships.

The Advocate Translator

The need to make sense of the irrational experience of sexual trauma is something that many attempt to do. Certainly trying to understand the trauma when it is your own experience is a process many survivors find difficult to avoid. The need to make sense of a behaviour that is experienced as being beyond explanation is even more difficult if your understanding is limited by impaired cognitive functioning. The advocate in the role of translator can however assist in the process of under-standing: providing clear information, interpreting symbolic behaviour and encouraging the survivor to express their own feelings and thoughts about what has happened. This can greatly improve the survivor's ability to assimilate what has occurred even if it is not possible to accept it. It is helpful for the advocate translator to be aware of some of the defences learning disabled survivors use against knowing the reality of what has occurred. It was Valerie Sinason who drew our attention to the use of learning disabled behaviour as a defence (Sinason, 1992). She refers to the existence of a secondary handicap, a handicap that has no organic foundation and is the result of trauma. The advocate translator will need to recognise the full implication of this as being that sexual abuse can be the primary cause of some aspects of 'handicapped' behaviour we see. Sinason states that 'the majority of the mildly mentally handicapped population have no organic brain damage, but environmentally they have experienced the worst that can be suffered'.

Respond's clinical experience confirms Sinason's observations. The behaviours that we see and define as handicapped, head banging, rocking to and fro, the person hitting, scratching and biting themselves, the person who continually screams and the person who continually smiles are not necessarily behaviours caused by the organic handicap, but are often responses directly related to trauma. The handicap is being used in the service of the self to protect it from unbearable memory of what is unbearable to know. The people we work with are often referred to as stupid, they give many examples of being referred to in this degrading manner. But behaviours like banging your head against the wall are stupid because they are causing pain when there need not be pain. It is a mad behaviour. Again Sinason provides essential insight for the advocate translator when she points out that the literal meaning of stupid reveals and illustrates the sense in stupid behaviour when usefully employed as a defence. Stupid means to become numb with grief. Knowing what our clients know has driven them to stupefy themselves as a defence. The behaviours we see are the outward signs and expressions of inner grief and human pain, and not necessarily symptoms of mental handicap.

It is the task of counsellor, psychotherapist and the advocate translator to recognise and understand the real meaning behind the presenting and confusing behaviours. When the advocate translator is able to translate freely and reflect to the survivor their understanding a liberation can occur and the survivor can be freed of their defences. This is a slow process and requires the advocate to be sensitive and cautious in their interpretations. Removing carefully constructed and intelligent defences must happen at the survivor's pace. Rapid deconstruction of defences by the advocate can leave the survivor feeling exposed and re-traumatised. Recognising defences and confused behaviours as a communication of what has happened and may be occurring in the survivor's inner world is the safest and most respectful task the advocate translator can provide.

The combined use of the witness, protester, nurturer and translator roles ensures that you can be there for the survivor of sexual abuse in the way that they require you to be. In many care settings these roles are already being fulfilled. It is easy to doubt what role you can play when faced with the overwhelming experience of sexual abuse. But the advocate roles enable us to be creative and responsive. More importantly they do not demand of the survivor 'what is wrong with you?' but rather 'what is wrong for you?'.

Feeling familiar and comfortable with these roles will help you to integrate them into your working practice. Reflecting on your own experiences of advocacy can be a helpful in facilitating your development as an advocate: who is it that fulfils the role of witness, protester, nurturer, and translator in your life? Who fulfils them in your work setting? And does your own personal experience of them differ from the experience of the people you are supporting? What do you need to bring the advocate roles into your life?

CHAPTER 3

Disclosure

Fahim, a young man with learning difficulties, had just finished telling how for 8 years his stepfather had been sexually abusing him. Now for the first time someone else knew. The relief was apparent in Fahim's expression and posture. His psychotherapist arranging to see him again moved towards the door. At this point Fahim stopped, turned and looked directly at his therapist. 'I've just given you the most horrible present in the world', he said. He then went on his way. 'I've just given you the most horrible present in the world': his words remained with the therapist not so much because of his ability to symbolise in such an intelligent way, but because of the powerful truth of his statement. Fahim was aware that the information he had given the therapist was indeed horrible in the extreme. It was information that he knew most people would rather not have. He also knew that once given it would not go away. Fahim's powerful statement contains some crucial indicators that we need to consider if we are in a position where we could be asked to receive the most horrible present in the world – the disclosure of sexual abuse.

One reason for the development of Respond was the recognition that when someone with a learning difficulty wanted to tell someone that they had been sexually abused they had nowhere to go. We recognised that for the victim of sexual abuse to become a survivor then the starting point was in the telling of what was happening or had happened to them and for there to be someone who could bear witness to their telling. The person who has been sexually abused has a unique need for a witness to their disclosure. Someone who will bear to know what they know to be true.In beginning to consider disclosure it is important to recognise the fact that sexual abuse is enshrouded in secrecy and denial. Secrecy is imposed by the perpetrator with a variety of intimidations that range from the subtle to the viciously sadistic. Fahim was shown a selection of knives by his abusing stepfather who told him that each knife would be used to dismember different parts of his body if he ever told anyone. Photographs of Jane's mother and younger sister were held up before her by her abusing uncle who then set fire to them as he told her that this would happen to them for real if she told anyone. In another case Paul was told that he was very special and that what happened between him and his abusing brother was so special that if anyone ever found out then they would both die. These examples illustrate how powerful methods used by abusers are in obtaining silence and maintaining secrecy. In view of this it is understandable that such sadistic silencing becomes so deeply internalised that childhood victims reach adulthood with the secret of the violations they have endured intact.

Such sadistic acts of silencing are carried out by abusers of adults who have learning difficulties. Many adults with learning difficulties are presenting in therapy details of their lives spent living in or using residential and day care services where there exists cultures of punishment hidden by silence. In these situations intimidation is used in the context of behaviour control. Here the perpetrator of sexual abuse can find well-established structures that support their need for silence. In such settings organised abuse rings can operate with relative freedom. If you were to examine the day-to-day practices of such establishments you would discover cultures of silence and fear. Cultures where people, providers and users are afraid to speak out.

Silence cannot be broken without the knowledge that there will be a witness. If secrecy is the mainstay of sexual abuse, then disclosure to a validating believing other is the first step in the process of healing and recovery. Appropriate responses to disclosures of sexual abuse need to become integrated into all levels of services; only then will the vulnerable life-styles of many people with learning difficulties be addressed.

Sadly many have divulged their secret previously, only to be met with disbelief, dismissal, rejection and in some cases abusive responses that mirror the original abuse. Responses such as 'It's in the past try to forget it' 'Did you enjoy it?' 'You were too little for it to have effect' 'Why didn't you tell someone' 'I can't bear for you to tell me' 'Do you really expect me to believe that' are common and result in the survivor feeling terrified of disclosing their abuse again for fear that they will be rejected.

Abusive responses indicate a very real resistance to receiving horrible information. As Fahim clearly understood, no one wants to receive such information. Understanding this resistance is important and requires us to make what is sometimes an uncomfortable assessment of our unwillingness to witness disclosure. At the core of resistance can often be found denial. Sexual abuse shakes our belief and the internal view we hold about society, family and humanity. Alice Miller in *Breaking Down the Walls of Silence* (1992) reminds us that throughout our lives we build high walls to defend ourselves from the painful knowledge that all is not what we would want it to be. Powerful influences in our society are also quick to defend this illusion especially in relation to sexual abuse. In the autumn of 1994 the response to professor La Fontain's report on the existence of satanic abuse was vitriolic in promoting her belief that it did not exist. However, those that have listened to survivors of such abuse cannot take comfort in such denial. The particular challenge of receiving a disclosure of sexual abuse makes a unique demand on our personal resources so much so that denial can appear an attractive option.

Some workers will have experienced silencing by others, in order to prevent them from being an able witness to disclosure, or there may be practices in our interaction with survivors that prevent us asking about abuse. Both indicate that it is not only the abused person who faces the difficulties of disclosure. Those who have a listening role face well-established problems. Long before the experiences of child care professionals in Cleveland (Butler-Sloss, 1988) the ability of service providers to be advocate witnesses was hindered. Having witnessed the effects of abuse Freud, who had recognised in his patients symptoms of trauma that indicated sexual abuse and initially spoke out about this, was intimidated into changing what he knew to be true (Krull, 1986; Masson, 1984). This pattern has been repeated through the years. Each time professions have been able to witness the reality of sexual abuse the response has been to deny, to turn away, discredit and abandon. In recent years qualified and experienced professionals throughout the world have all met with disbelief and outrage. The very tools that we have developed to enable people to tell us about what has happened to them have also been discredited: anatomical dolls, the use of art work and even now the video link have all been questioned. The witnessing ability of counselling and therapy is constantly attacked. The pressure not to bear witness to a disclosure is great.

Practices in our personal and daily interaction with clients can also prevent disclosure and can unconsciously act to prevent us from being an effective witness. The recording of a personal history seldom includes enquiries about uncomfortable or difficult sexual experiences. Presenting challenging behaviours requiring vast amounts of time and energy are managed without questioning the root cause. There is a repeated failure to enquire into the existence of previous or ongoing sexual trauma. Sometimes indicators of abuse such as vaginal discharge, physical injury and sexually transmitted diseases are responded to without the question of the possibility of assault or abuse being raised.

The specialist worker, psychotherapist and counsellor may also resist asking about sexual abuse; or, if they do pose questions, they may not take into account the non-verbal responses that can be triggered by such questioning. Non-verbal responses are often the expression of repressed abuse trauma, experiences that the client has dissociated from and therefore cannot verbalise. The experience of abuse is then communicated consciously in the physical response. Gordon would sit week by week talking about his life with no reference to his past abuse. When asked if the time was right for him to tell about the things his mother had done to him, he would start to rock violently in his chair and to bite his arm. These behaviours had been present for many years, his file recorded these behaviours on a regular basis, but only in connection to and as evidence of his learning difficulty. These self-injurious behaviours were not symptomatic of any organic deficit. However, they were clear indicators of inner psychic pain related to the repeated trauma of sexual abuse.

Some survivors who seek help about all sorts of things are desperate to talk about their abuse but may not unless and until they know the therapist or helper is willing and able to hear them and be their witness.

Assessing our willingness to be an effective witness to disclosure is not easy. Challenging the myths we hold about sexual abuse and examining our own attitudes can be painful especially if our beliefs are supported by our professional status and power. It is not that unusual to find within service settings the myth that sexual abuse never happens or that sexual abuse only occurs in certain communities, cultures or classes. Other myths are not uncommon in professional settings. Myths concerning responsibility for the sexual abuse, such as children are sexually provocative; sexual abuse is the produce of dysfunctional families; and because the victim has learning difficulties then it doesn't matter anyway. Advice given by an officer in charge of a home for young people with learning difficulties to a residential social worker who had reported her suspicions of sexual abuse was to 'turn a blind eye, it must have been going on for ages, anyway'. Implying that because it had been going on for a long time then it did not merit concern. This is an example of double abuse: not only is the possible existence of sexual abuse being ignored but the dismissive response also indicates the low value attributed to the life of the learning disabled person.

There are also personal issues that can hinder the would-be effective witness and further indicate the need for supervision and emotional support. Witnessing disclosure can facilitate memories of the worker's own abusive experiences. Particular issues may be raised concerning the gender and sexuality of the worker as well as the range of feelings and emotions that accompany the process of hearing including feelings of guilt, fear, anger, rage, shock, horror, dread, grief, sadness, disgust, distress, sexual arousal and the desire to rescue.

The task facing the witness to believe, see, hear and validate is not complex but, as the range of emotive responses illustrated in this chapter indicate, there is a need to be prepared. There is a preliminary to supporting the survivor in this way and that involves possible witnesses asking – 'Do I feel prepared?' 'Do I feel ready?' 'Do I have adequate support?' 'Do I have adequate supervision?'. And service managers need to ask 'Are staff prepared and ready and what can we do to ensure they are?' 'Do we provide adequate support?' and 'Do we provide adequate supervision?'. The witness has a need for policy that embraces these important questions. Such a policy need not necessarily provide a step-by-step account of what to do and say, but it should aim to enable the worker to give the message that 'Yes it is possible for you to respond to the person who has been sexually abused and you will not be left on your own whilst you are responding'.

A supported witness will be able to give effective messages to the survivor. These messages need to be explicit and implicit and they should form the basis of our communications at the point of disclosure and following. The messages include 'I believe you' 'It's not your fault' 'I'm glad you told me' 'I'm sorry this happened to you' 'I'm going to help you'.

Belief

'I believe you': the ability to offer belief is central to supporting the survivor of sexual abuse. Witnessing someone telling you what has happened to them, and what has been done to them, is not the same as conducting an investigation. As an advocate witness you are able to offer belief in the reality as it is presented to you at that moment in time. This is very different from a legal investigation where the emphasis is on obtaining substantiated facts. The advocate witness is able to listen free from this obligation. Unconditional belief in the survivor's reality as it is presented to you is one of the most important factors in relation to the healing process.

When survivors enter therapy many sessions can be spent working with the effects of not being believed. Alex was 17 years old when he first came for therapy. He had a learning difficulty and had been sexually and physically abused by his father and some of his father's friends since the age of 11. At different stages in his life he had told people whom he thought could help him: a neighbour, a teacher and his priest. The inability of these people to believe what Alex told them resulted in Alex being victimised again and again for a further 7 years. Alex required 26 sessions of therapy before he could even begin to speak in the sessions and a further year of weekly appointments before he could tell about the abuse. For a while Alex experienced the disbelief of those he initially believed could help him as the greater abuse.

'I believe you' needs to be communicated in our words, posture and actions. Alex is not alone; any hint of disbelief following such an experience will be recognised by the sensitised survivor. Questions asking for clarification, changes in voice tone and expression can all be interpreted by the survivor as disbelief. The experience of not being believed can maintain survivors in the original silence, and disbelief can drive survivors into madness. When you know a terrible reality and there is an absence of a believing other the doubt that is brought to bear on the reality is overwhelming; madness in such a situation is an intelligent defence. The belief of others in what we know to be real is essential in maintaining our sense of self and good mental health.

Guilt

'It's not your fault': Lea on hearing that his father had just been given a prison sentence for sexually abusing him, said 'I'm so glad he's behind bars but it's not over. I feel it was all my fault, what can I do about it?' Talking about guilt with Lea revealed that he held a belief that all that had happened to him was his fault and that something about him had caused him to be sexually abused. Eventually he was able to explain that he believed that because he had a learning difficulty his father had chosen him and not his two brothers to abuse. He also said that his father had blamed him saying that if he had been good like the others then there would have been no need for the abuse to happen. Perpetrators will use blame to ensure silence with the result that if the abuse occurs in childhood the survivor grows up with an internalised belief that it is all their fault. For the survivor with learning difficulties this guilt is compounded by an awareness that they are different. The following statements were made in a group of men with learning difficulties who had all experienced sexual abuse: 'I have a learning difficulty, there is something wrong with me, it must have been my fault' 'This happened to me because I have a learning difficulty – it is my fault the way I am'. These beliefs are present in many learning disabled survivors. The advocate, counsellor and therapist must ensure that internalised beliefs are explored in relation to both the experience of sexual abuse and the experience of having a learning disability.

Guilt is experienced because of the abuse itself, and because of the disclosure with its resulting consequences, especially if there has been an investigation or if the family have been separated or associated people distanced from the survivor's life. There are many losses associated with times of disclosure, and the guilt that follows these experiences if not addressed can lead to depression, increased self-harming behaviour and to suicide.

The worker witnessing disclosure may be the first person who is able to give the message 'you're not to blame', 'you are not guilty', 'it is not your fault'. These messages need to permeate all interactions with the survivor.

Security

'I'm glad you told me': when Fahim left his therapist with the most horrible present the therapist recognised that Fahim looked relaxed. Because he had not been rejected by the therapist he was able to pain there was also the new knowledge that someone was still there for him despite the awfulness of his trauma. The therapist, by acknowledging the difficulty Fahim experienced in disclosing and then stating that he was glad Fahim felt able to tell him, offered a sense of security at a time that was fraught with the risk of abandonment.

'I told my mum and she shouted at me' is a statement heard many times when survivors explain the reactions they receive when they first disclose. Such responses create feelings of shame and in some cases lead to rejection and abandonment eventually creating further vulnerability: Gordon, who was abused at the hands of a paedophile ring, was thrown out of his carers home 'we did not want him in the house' they explained to his social worker. Gordon moved on into prostitution and substance abuse. 'I'm glad you told me' is a simple message indicating hope and an opportunity for justice. As is apparent in Gordon's case, when this message is not given the consequences can be disastrous.

Empathy

'I'm sorry this happened to you': this empathic response reinforces to the survivor that they have made the right choice in telling and acts to counter any doubt or fear that they may be feeling. We should not underestimate the presence of fear at the point of disclosure especially if the survivor has been involved in ritual, satanic, cult or organised abuse. These forms of abuse often use fear as a means of control (Tate, 1991). Fiona had been hypnotised and programmed to suicide by a satanic coven. When she told of her abuse a symbol acting as a trigger was sent to her and she presented in several sessions as suicidal. As with all satanic abuse she had internalised a belief system that completely reversed the common good: she believed all that had happened to her was the right thing to have happened, and those who were attempting to stop it were bad. 'I'm sorry this has happened to you' was a powerful new message for her and needed to be a constant message not only throughout her disclosure but also throughout her following treatment.

Support

'I'm going to help you': the witness to disclosure in stating this implies that there is an end in sight, that help is possible and that the survivor is no longer alone. It requires the witness to be practical in giving consideration to their future role, especially if an investigation follows.

An investigation will involve many other people. Professionals that are not known by the survivor will be drawn into the proceedings and the advocate witness may find him or herself pushed aside. This can have a devastating effect for the survivor who for many good reasons selects with care the witness. There is no reason why the witness cannot remain alongside the survivor throughout the investigation. Once the investigation is over care is required to maintain a supportive presence as this can be a particularly vulnerable time for the survivor. So often the end of an investigation is seen by others as the end of the matter, but for the survivor it is just the beginning. If the advocate witness can still be available and involved in developing ongoing support then this will be a valuable contribution to the healing process that will continue beyond disclosure.

Following Disclosure

The witness who is able to give these messages will in doing so facilitate the early stages of healing and recovery. The positive outcomes of disclosure are many, but we also need to recognise that breaking the abuse secret has an effect on the survivor which can be challenging for them and all involved. Appropriate support will need to be accessed. It is not unusual following disclosure for the survivor to experience flashbacks or re-enactments of the trauma or to display self-punitive behaviour all evoked by the betrayal of and disloyalty to the abuser represented by the act of the disclosure itself.

Anna following a detailed disclosure during therapy returned to subsequent sessions with lacerations to her wrists and legs. Following this the staff in her residential unit were ringing the therapist saying that the therapy was making her depressed and that they wanted to stop it. It was important for the therapist to state that such a reaction following disclosure is temporary and is a response to repressed memories and feelings resurfacing and becoming conscious. Remembering is painful and signals to us that one disclosed incident of abuse is seldom an isolated incident but the beginning of what can be several months of the disclosure of new information involving many other abuses.

Recovery from the trauma of sexual abuse commences at the point of disclosure. The process can be long and complex. The nature and quality of the immediate response, however, should be simple. Understanding what it is like for the survivor to give the most horrible present in the world, being aware of the possible consequences and developing a witnessing response is how we can best start to support the survivor of sexual trauma.

Working with suspicion

Not all experiences of sexual abuse are disclosed in a clear and obvious manner. It is not unusual for survivors of abuse not to speak about their experiences until many years after the abuse has stopped. The trauma of abuse can therefore remain hidden, even to the survivor, until an event in their life triggers an association. Such triggers can come from a range of experiences and events such as new experiences of adult relationships, changes in the abuser's life or the survivor's mother's life, in the lives of the survivor's siblings and the presence of children. Other abusive situations can also trigger memories of past abuse along with experiences of loss, medical examinations and procedures, changes in employment, involvement with professional services and awareness of media coverage. Being aware of these possible triggers will enable workers to recognise the possible significance of specific changes in behaviour or emotional expression within the people they are caring for.

Not all triggers will result in behaviour and emotion that indicate sexual abuse but it is wise to question what is being communicated in various presenting behaviours and changes in emotional expression. Working with people with learning disabilities it is easy to become familiar with extreme forms of behaviour and expression. Given the high incident of sexual abuse indicated in research by Brown *et al* (1994) and in our own clinical findings we can no longer think that all presenting behaviours have their cause in the organic learning disability. Indeed many behaviours presented to us are attempts to communicate a range of traumatic experiences both past and present.

Signs and symptoms that can indicate sexual abuse include any combination of the long-term effects (see Figure 3.1) and also any combination of the following:

- Previous psychiatric history with several different diagnoses and still not much better.
- No memories of childhood/over-positive description of childhood.
- Significant behaviour disturbance.
- Running away.
- Persistent urinary tract infections.
- Withdrawal or isolation from peer group.
- Pronounced fear of individuals.
- Self-mutilation or injury, including head banging.
- Indiscriminate/inappropriate sexual behaviour.
- Fear of intimacy.
- Unexplained physical complaint.

- Recurring dissociation.
- Intrusive obsessions and phobias.
- Unexplained injuries.
- Compulsive erotic behaviour.
- Acting out sexual acts.
- Sudden extreme fear of the bathroom, bathing, water, rain.
- Nightmares, terrors and sweats.
- Hyper-aggressiveness.
- Sudden eating disorders.
- Fear of darkness.
- Vomiting for no apparent reason.
- Drawings of signs, symbols and violent acts.

Recognition of any combination of these signs and symptoms should give rise to suspicion and prompt an assessment of the presenting signs and symptoms.

Workers also report having an intuitive sense that someone is being sexually abused and sometimes suspicions are reported by another person or agency. Before taking any action a thorough assessment of the suspicion is essential. The assessment should be conducted where possible by those who have a good holistic knowledge of the person in question. If the suspicion indicates that the individual is in immediate danger practical interventions may need to be implemented to remove the person to a safe place. Further investigation can take place once the safety and well-being of the person has been secured. However, care should be taken to ensure that suspicions are carefully assessed and this process does take time. A rushed assessment will only result in vague and undefined outcomes and will hinder any interventions that may be required at a later date. Taking time to plan the assessment will help to keep the investigation focused on the person and will help to prevent inappropriate interventions.

Signs and symptoms that are a cause for concern broadly fall into three categories:

1. Physical indicators.

2. Behavioural indicators.

3. Social/other indicators (SCOSAC, 1991).

The suspicions causing concern should be considered to see what category of indicators are present. Once defined this should be stated clearly and without adding further explanation or interpretation.

In the next phase of the assessment the worker is required to bring together as complete a picture as possible of the life of the person who the suspicions are about. All the following areas require exploration so that a full history can be compiled and compared with present-day events. The areas for exploration need to include personal history, race and cultural identity and practices, the nature and manifestation of organic learning disability, family background and interactions with the wider community. As each category is explored it can become apparent that little is known about some areas of the client's lives. It is vital that gaps in our knowledge be noted and opportunities found to ensure that we can locate others who can help provide any missing information. Whilst the overall profile is being developed care should be taken to identify key people in each category who will have a wider or more in-depth knowledge of the particular areas where information is required.

Once all the information is gathered each suspicion should be considered against each area of the complete profile. The assessor needs to ask what possible causes are there for each indicator other than sexual abuse and who can provide a check for the possible reasons. The result for each conclusion should be recorded. It may be possible to convene a professional networking meeting to help with this process. If the process of elimination provides and confirms satisfactory answers to the suspicion then no further action would be necessary. If, however, the suspicions remain unanswered or information cannot confirm safety then a formal investigation would need to be instigated.

Policy and guidelines

As services seek to respond to disclosures of sexual abuse comprehensive policy development is essential. A good policy will address the process of assessing suspicion and provide a clear investigation procedure. Many concerns are raised during assessment and investigation at the centre of which is the suspected victim or confirmed survivor. Careful management of both suspicion and confirmed disclosure is essential in respecting his or her difficult position and long-term welfare.

CHAPTER 4

The Relevance of Attachment and Loss

In 1988, as part of a counselling training, I watched a film (Robertson, 1952) about a little boy aged 20 months who had been sent to live in a nursery for 10 days while his mother had a new baby. This was a period when there were few expectations that fathers would interrupt their working lives to care for children. Placing the child in organised care for what was, after all, such a short time was felt to be a sensible way of ensuring that the mother did not have to try and look after a toddler as well as give birth to new baby.

This film, made by the Robertson's as part of their research into the effects of separation on young children, had an extraordinarily powerful effect on me. We watched as this little boy, who had never before been apart from his mother for so much as day, struggled to make sense of his new surroundings. At first he was fine – after all nothing disturbing had happened to him before and he had no reason to believe that his mother would not come back. Later on that first day he became unhappy and tearful. When his father came to visit him that evening he was very upset and clung on to his father, angry when he, too, tried to leave. The next day he was miserable and tried hard to get attention from a particular nursery nurse. She didn't have time to devote exclusively to him and anyway, the next day she was not on duty. He was angry again when his father visited that day, and his father was clearly uncomfortable as he did not even take his coat off. Over the next few days the little boy went into a decline. He literally gave up. He made some attempts to form a bond with one of the film makers who was observing (and who was, of course, a consistent presence) and he found an enormous teddy bear which he lay on the floor and cuddled. He refused to make eye contact with his father and rejected his attempts to cuddle him. At the time I was struck by just how little time it took for this boy to give up the fight, just how lost he was without the presence of a consistent, loving and supportive person who could understand him and put him first. The shock he felt at the transformation which had taken place in his life was palpable. His pain was literally unbearable for many of those watching. We were a large audience and there was not much opportunity for feedback. But my colleagues spoke of powerful memories from their own childhood which had been evoked, and of renewed, or first-time guilt at separations they had subjected their own children to. There was a widespread longing to know what had happened to the boy in the future and to know that he was all right – that long-term damage had not occurred.

What was the source of this film's power and why is it so relevant to the work we are doing at Respond today?

It was so affecting because to some extent it had happened to all of us there. We have all had an infancy, and that infancy has been characterised by our relationship with our primary care givers. We have all experienced, at some time, the pain of rejection, and of loss and abandonment. We have all needed to be held, to be loved unconditionally regardless of whether we are happy or sad, easy or difficult. We have needed to look into our parents' eyes and see reflected in them their belief that we are beautiful.

Sometimes it is hard to face the pain of another person's experiences of loss because we are reminded so clearly of our own. We shun contact with those who have been newly bereaved, for example, or are confused by the fury a client feels towards us when we are going away on holiday. Each new separation evokes painful ones from the past. Anger at an abandoning parent is expressed as anger at the therapist. There is scarcely an aspect of our current work at Respond which is not illuminated and more clearly understood by considering it in the light of what we know about attachment.

In structuring our service, we emphasise the significance of the relationship between therapists and clients. We make it clear that this relationship will take time to form and that when it has it must be respected. Therapy represents an opportunity for a new and secure attachment to form for clients. By valuing and respecting the clients, by always keeping the therapeutic space clear for them and their issues, the clients can experience the safety of being held. They can be appreciated for who they are. They can behave in ways which will test the relationship to its limits. They can have the first chance ever to be the one who does the abandoning, by choosing to leave therapy. Our primary task is not to reject the client. We know that clients may experience difficulties at times of enforced separation. We recognise and respect the importance of early-life experiences. For many of our clients, their early life is a closed chapter and yet it contains keys to understanding their life now. We help clients feel safe to begin to explore the past, although this is often painful and many hurt and angry feelings surface as a result.

John Bowlby, who is the originator of Attachment Theory, believed that the early relationships in our lives were crucial to our future emotional well-being. He saw the damage that was caused to children when these early relationships were not strong, safe and consistent ones and attributed many problems encountered later in life to these earlier broken attachments.

When we began working at Respond we thought that we would be working with the aftermath of abuse, often experienced by our clients when they were adults. We knew they would be traumatised, shocked and frightened. We would provide a safe, containing space for the expression of these feelings. What we have come to realise that at the heart of each experience of sexual abuse is a relationship and that the nature of the relationship between abuser and victim will have profound effects on the victim. We now also know that very many of our clients are referred because of a known incident of abuse which has occurred in adulthood but that the material presented and worked with is about much earlier experiences and especially about families. (Although not the focus of this book, we are also addressing the connection between an early history of broken attachments and later offending behaviour.) This is not an academic book and we want to present Attachment Theory in a way which is related closely to our everyday work. The following case histories are shared with the intention of doing this.

Tracy came to our project when she was 32. A woman with mild learning disabilities, and the mother of three children, she was about to see the two youngest, a girl and boy, join her eldest in the care of the local authority. Her social worker felt that she was giving up her children with too little resistance and wanted her to advocate more strongly in defence of herself as a mother. Tracy bristled with anger as soon as she came into Respond. She was angry with everyone in a position of authority. This included social workers, doctors, teachers at her children's school, and people who worked in the local library. All of these people had let her down in hundreds of ways. Mostly they let her down because they could not be her parents. They could not look after her in the way that she needed to be looked after. Tracy had never known her father. He had left the family home when Tracy was a young child and she had no idea where he was now. In her mind he was a wonderful, caring and loving man who would never treat her badly. Tracy's mother no longer spoke to her.

Indeed the only positive times of contact between them were when Tracy had had her own babies and her mother had come to visit. Tracy told me that when she was a child her mother had neglected her, left her alone, locked her in a room without food or water and failed to protect her from the bullying of her older brother and sister and the sexual abuse of her stepfather. Tracy says that everyone in her family hated her and everybody wished she had not been born. The exception was her grandmother who had been supportive but was now refusing to see her after a big row. Tracy's eldest child, now aged 11, was received into care when she was sexually abused by Tracy's then partner. Her two youngest children were deemed to be at risk from her current partner.

Tracy did not attend therapy for very long but in the short time that we worked together I saw how she longed to be close to people and that being pregnant and having babies provided her with this closeness. Her neediness meant she was unable to keep her children safe, but it was clear that she loved her children fiercely. She felt extremely isolated and recognised that her relationships with men did not satisfactorily counter this isolation. Because her children were at risk, they had become the focus of everyone's attention and once again, Tracy was rejected – her own needs not met. It was important that, as Tracy's counsellor, I did not have contact with her children and could operate independently of child protection services. Of course the children had to be kept safe, but Tracy needed someone who was there just for her. I worked with Tracy to make connections between the anger and hurt she felt now and the loneliness and vulnerability she had felt as a child. I witnessed with her the pain of her childhood and protested at the injustices she had suffered. Tracy received excellent support from a family centre and was able to end her relationship with her partner and keep care of the children. Tracy's history was one of longing for attachment with people who loved her. Because she had had support from her grandmother she knew what it could be like and she knew what she wanted to provide for children from inside herself. Her own needs for protection had never been met and she was not able at first to protect her own children. The Family Centre provided security and boundaries for Tracy and her relationship with me offered the chance for her early attachment deprivation to be recognised and worked with. I did not judge her.

Tracy's case illustrates that sexual abuse in childhood can make people more vulnerable to being abused. It isn't possible to make guarantees of safety and to rid the world of sex offenders. But a healthily attached child grows up knowing that someone cares what happens to it and will speak out when bad things happen. If you are securely attached to your child, her pain will be your pain so of course you will act to protect her from hurt. We know that offenders target their victims very carefully and that they are drawn to people who they perceive to be vulnerable. As one perpetrator said, in relation to his abuse of children in public parks, 'I never go for the flash ones – the ones that look intelligent'. Tracy lacked people who minded what happened to her and she lacked the inner strength which is bestowed by a knowledge that you matter to people. Secure attachments give a secure base from which to function in the world. If you do not have to worry about sustaining supporting relationships, you will be free to explore the world. You will have the sense that there is a safe place for you to return to, that it will always be there for you when you need it. A toddler, just learning to move about independently of its mother, will go so far before turning around to check that its mother is still there. Beyond a certain point, the bond between them, serving rather like an invisible piece of elastic which connects them, becomes overstretched and the child must return for reassurance.

If you are anxious about your relationships, you will be frightened to leave them unattended. And the power of attachment bonds is that they become more noticeable when under stress. So the child who is being treated badly by its parents will cling on all the harder, for fear of losing them altogether, often tolerating terrible abuse so as not to break the attachment. If children are separated from their abusing parents, they will need to mourn the loss of the parent.

Alice was emotionally, sexually and physically abused by her mother and eventually removed from the family home. She remembers the abuse clearly and was told that her mother was unable to care for her properly. She has spent many months in therapy trying to understand the fact that she may never see her mother again and says often that she loved her and wants to see her. She is supervised to the extent that contact is unlikely to occur and yet the loss of a kind and loving mother who could care for her remains as Alice's main preoccupation. On the rare occasions when she receives a letter from her mother, she will bring it to therapy and study every word as if searching for meaning and insight into her abandonment.

Barbara has had a relationship with a non-learning disabled man who has been a friend of the family for many years. She is deeply attached to him but feels pressured into having sex with him. Although she talks about this pressure and has even been to the police on one occasion, she has always stopped herself from pursuing a complaint because she does not want to lose her relationship with him. Ourselves and other people who care for Barbara must act if we feel Barbara is in danger, but her learning disabilities do not preclude her consenting to sex. We must work to empower Barbara to be able to resist the pressure for sex, but we must also recognise the strength of her attachment to her boyfriend.

Linda regularly met men in cafés or on public transport and took them back to her flat where they often sexually abused her. She was lonely and wanted to make contact with men. A lifetime in institutions had given her little opportunity to do this through any medium other than abusive sex. Unless Linda was going to return to the confines of a hospital it was difficult to prevent her from making these contacts – her desire for human contact eclipsed the demands made by her key worker to 'not talk to strangers'. Each time, she felt there was potential for closeness and this overrode concerns for her physical safety. After each abuse she was traumatised and distressed, requiring much more support from those caring for her. Perhaps she was also testing all of us. Linda is involved with her local church, and as time went on, it was support from long-standing caring members of the congregation, which seemed to counter her need to put herself in risky situations. In therapy, she was not judged for her behaviour or told what to do or not do. Instead we worked together to understand what feelings drove her actions. Perhaps it is this opportunity – to feel that you belong somewhere and that people care for you – combined with therapy which gives a space and safety to explore difficult feelings which can help to build a sense of secure attachments.

Bowlby recognised that a significant aspect of a secure attachment was that a child could express its negative emotions as well as its positive ones – that protest was healthy and necessary and should not be silenced. Many of our clients have had to work hard to suppress negative emotions because no one in their life makes room for them. Mary talks constantly about her sister and her two daughters and about how much she loves them and how wonderful they are. She also fantasises about taking a baby from its mother, or from a maternity hospital. Sometimes she imagines that she is pregnant, or being sterilised or she becomes extremely distressed whilst talking about the fact she will never have children. She cannot express these feelings to her family as to do so may threaten her relationship with her sister and nieces but neither can she banish her own powerful feelings of jealousy and loss. In therapy these are given room for expression.

In his book, *John Bowlby and Attachment Theory* (1993), Holmes considers how caring institutions can work to provide a secure base for their residents and he identifies what should be present for them to do so.

- Does the resident have someone to turn to who is specifically orientated towards their needs?
- Are the resident's basic physiological and physical health needs adequately catered for?
- Are the resident's needs to love and hate recognised?
- Are there clear limits against which the residents can test strength and weakness, and learn to differentiate between fantasy and reality?

At the core of much abuse we find attachment issues and we need to recognise these and address them in our provision of services.

Bowlby and those who have continued with Attachment-based work, such as Mary Ainsworth and Mary Main, have found much material through observing the behaviour elicited by separation. Indeed this is the basis of Mary Ainsworth's (1978) *Strange Situation*, as described by Holmes (1993) which is used as a tool to assess the type of attachment between mothers and infants. Bowlby saw that separation anxiety was a realistic response to separation or threatened separation and its key features are:

- a subjective feeling of worry, pain and tension;
- angry protest to register displeasure at the leaving person and to punish them so they won't do it again;
- a restless searching for the missing person.

Later, Bowlby explored the consequences of a permanent separation when a loved-one dies (Bowlby, 1980; Holmes, 1993). This work provides helpful insight when considering sexual abuse in terms of the losses endured by victims.

There are many such losses when a person is sexually abused. They may lose any or all of the following, depending on the individual circumstances:

- innocence
- childhood
- normality
- parents and other family members
- a sex life which is pleasurable
- their home
- joy
- ordinary and open friendships.

We have found it helpful to consider the feelings and behaviour of our clients in the context of a mourning process. We recognise that this process will not be moved through in a straightforward way, from one phase and thence on to another, and also that to reach the point of 'moving on' may take a very long time.

We have identified these parts of the mourning process in material presented to us by Respond clients:

- Numbness.
- Denial.
- Yearning and searching.
- Anger.
- Weeping and wailing.
- Realisation.
- Remembering and reminiscing.
- Synthesis.
- Moving on.

Numbness

This may be the initial reaction to a bereavement or loss – a shutting-down of the emotions until it is safe to express feeling. Sometimes that time of safety may not arrive for years. This will be true if a person is trapped in an abusive situation for years with nobody or no means of telling what is happening. When Christine first came to Respond she told me her life story – she described being abandoned by her mother as a baby, abused within and then rejected by her foster family, staying in a number of children's homes from which she absconded or was removed, living rough and having sex to get a bed for the night and being physically abused by the men she had sex with. Eventually Christine went to live in a long-stay hospital and she was sexually abused there. She had no family and contact with only one person who she had met outside the hospital. She had known no one else for longer than 4 years. As she talked, Christine showed no feelings at all. She could have been reading me that evening's television programmes from the *Radio Times*. Christine wasn't denying that these terrible things had occurred to her, but she could not permit herself to feel the consequences of them.

Denial

Grace, who came voluntarily to a group for women who had all been abused by a member of staff, spent many weeks denying that anything bad had happened to her. Until she had developed trust in the members and process of the group, she could not admit what she had experienced.

Our clients receive many messages to reinforce their denial. For example, that what happened wasn't so bad, or that your parents should be loved whatever the circumstances.

Often denial is accompanied by an idealisation of the abuser. If the victim can convince herself that her abuser is in fact a wonderful person then this will make her abuse an impossibility. John had been abused over a period of 10 years by a teacher at his special school. Because this man was one of the few people to ever demonstrate a commitment to John, and show an interest in him, John felt very positively towards him. He also gave John lots of presents and John himself never disclosed the abuse.

Yearning and searching

Loss and bereavement may be accompanied by a restlessness and a searching – literally to find the lost person who has died. For a sexually abused person, this may be the search to find the non-abusing parent they didn't have, or for their own identity beneath all the confusion. Alan was regularly anally abused by his brother. His learning disabilities were severe and his speech confused. Alan lost things a lot – his wallet, his bus pass, his pencils, his coat. Each episode of losing caused him great distress. Surely these small losses, endlessly repeated, represented his struggle to make sense of the larger loss he had suffered.

Alice goes over and over the events of her childhood as if searching for the moment at which it went wrong and turned into a story of abuse and neglect. Sometimes she talks as though she has found it – 'It was when my Mum fell down the stairs' or 'It was when my mum got ill because my dad hit her'.

Anger

Many of our clients show us that they are angry about what has happened to them. Often this anger is not attached to its source and is not expressed in a safe or acceptable way. We have found that an opportunity to express quite justified anger can be a great motor to healing. Tracy (see above) was furious in her approach to her life and this helped her to feel strong and more in control of her dreadful circumstances. Her anger was also exhausting for her and destructive too as it sabotaged her relationships with anyone who tried to help. Often they couldn't, but often Tracy's expectations of them were unrealistic and therapy helped her to understand this.

Kate was sexually and physically abused by her father in a very violent way and it has made Kate very angry. Sometimes she will turn her anger on people who are trying to support her; for example by stealing from her friends or by attacking her carers. At other times she is able to be in therapy and shout at her absent father, berating him and telling him what she feels about the terrible things he has done. Kate has not been rejected by her new carers, who can understand her behaviour and although she is testing them a lot of the time, she is also beginning to understand that she is allowed her anger but that she should not hurt other people because she is so angry.

Weeping and Wailing

It may be that therapy is the only opportunity that a client has to feel the awfulness of what has happened and to express their great sadness. These times can be hard for the supporter because they may feel that they have made the victim feel worse. Kate will often spend a large part of each session sobbing. If we can stay with her, and allow her to cry, she is able to stop and say that she feels better afterwards.

Jane, who felt terribly betrayed when she found out that her abuser had abused other residents as well as her – she had thought she was the only one – became very upset in a session. Using a disclosure doll to represent her abuser, she punched and kicked him, jumped on him and pulled his hair, crying loudly throughout. Until that point she had presented as a person who was coping very well, and denying that she had been affected.

This was clearly not the case as she also found it hard to get out of bed each day, lost her temper a great deal, and sabotaged many positive relationships.

Realisation

One week, Tracy brought a large pile of pictures to the session with her, clipped from women's magazines. All were glossy and coloured and depicted mothers with their children, or children playing happily with beautiful toys. All except one picture – a fund-raising advertisement for a children's charity. This was a grainy, black and white image, showing a sad child sitting alone on the steps of a house. Tracy said, 'This is my favourite because this one shows what it was like for me when I was a child'.

Although initially this realisation can be very painful and lead to renewed sadness at the losses experienced, if it does not occur the victim will not develop a true understanding of his or her experiences. Bowlby believed that this clear narrative was a crucial part of the way in which a child can grow up to feel secure inside. This is now widely recognised within adoption agencies who no longer tell adoptive families to pretend that the adoptive child had no life before they came to them. Instead the child has a life-story book, in which the truth of their background is not hidden.

Josie is 18. Sexually abused by both her parents within an abuse ring, and also physically abused by her mother with whom she now has no contact she says, 'I haven't got a real mother any more. She treated me badly'.

Remembering and Reminiscing

After realisation it is as though a clear outline picture of a victim's experiences is available to them and their memories will colour the picture in full. These may be memories which have been buried for many years and may emerge slowly over a long period of time. It is very important that time is allowed for this process and that the supporter is able to listen and help the victim make sense of what they remember. Alice knew that her brother's friend had forced her to have sex with him when she was a child of 10. Recently she has been remembering other instances of brutality and abuse perpetrated by these young men – of being teased, pushed around and locked in a room.

She remembers the confusing and mad behaviour of her mother, who would take her clothes off in public, or leave Alice unsupervised for many hours. She has also remembered when her mother complained to the school that Alice was being treated unfairly by a teacher, and when she and her mother went shopping together to buy food for the family.

Synthesis

Alice is beginning to achieve a synthesis. She has a clear picture of the good and the bad things which have happened to her. There is no way of undoing the bad things, of having a childhood in which they did not occur. With synthesis, Alice will be able to recognise that good and bad have made her who she is today and to move on from the confusion that she feels about herself. This confusion has made relationships very difficult for Alice. She has had to close down so many of her emotions to be able to live with the pain of her early experiences, that she has become very distant from people.

Moving On

As a victim becomes stronger and more self-aware, he or she will be able to move on, and no longer need the prop and supports that sustained them throughout the mourning process. Indeed, they may reject what was once helpful because it is an uncomfortable reminder of earlier distress. When Tracy was able to move back into her flat with her children she did not return to Respond. Linda sends us a Christmas card each year.

CHAPTER 5

Core Issues

The stage that follows disclosure is the beginning of the journey towards recovery and healing from trauma. This may occur within the clinical consulting room with a trained psychotherapist, it may happen in the group home television room with a trusted keyworker, it may take place on the journey to the day centre with a friendly and sensitive care assistant. Wherever the location and whatever the relationship, it is important to stress the continuing need for the supporter of the survivor of sexual abuse to see beyond the explicit behaviours demonstrated by the client through to the implicit communication they are attempting to make.

When attempting to look beyond the external manifestations of trauma we invariably find ourselves accessing a set of core issues which, if not addressed, threaten to divert us from the central aim of recognising the survivor's experience of abuse in favour of seeking merely to treat the symptoms. It is especially true of working with people with learning disabilities that many services operate in response to symptoms rather than root causes. In the case of sexual abuse, these symptoms may be nightmares, sleep disturbance, self-injuring, uncontrolled aggression or inappropriate sexual behaviour. It is tempting in most cases for these symptoms to be treated in too behaviourist a short-term manner. Behaviour modification charts may seem the sensible measure when confronted with a client who is constantly slashing her arms when distressed. In many cases the modification may control or erase the behaviour. What we tend to discover, however, is that a new challenging behaviour simply replaces the arm slashing. The underlying reason for the initial behaviour may be addressed only by seeking to investigate the root cause.

In this chapter we will look at a series of core issues present in the lives of many of the clients worked with by Respond. The set of core issues may alter with each client you find yourself working with, but what does not change is the need to work at this deeper level. The ability to bear to delve below the surface is paramount in the ability to facilitate therapeutic change.

'Damaged Goods Syndrome'

Our clients have used many creative communication tools to evoke in the listener the experience of living a life with the constant realisation of indigenous difference. A feeling of inherent alienation we term 'damaged goods syndrome'. When looking at the early life experiences of people with learning disabilities, it is difficult not to be struck by the difficulties inherent in early emotional development. Society has never been good at valuing people with learning disabilities so it is not surprising that parents who face the challenge of having a child with any kind of disability carry with them a set of emotional responses which may not be so present in the parents of a non-disabled infant. Those Respond clients who have been able to approach their memories of early childhood have almost unanimously communicated memories of insecure attachments which had fed into an underpinning lack of self-esteem. One client we have worked with struggled before and after his sexual abuse with a feeling he described as 'Like a monster that looked back at me in the mirror. Ever since I was little. An ugly monster.'

There are, of course, those parents who have been able to integrate and deal healthily with the feelings of fear, shock, horror and rejection which accompany the birth of a child deemed by society as not being a valid human being, as being bereft of the basic values of humanity we ascribe to children without disabilities. Many parents, however, struggle with these overwhelming reactions and communicate them, consciously or unconsciously, to their offspring. The work of psychotherapists such as Daniel Stern and John Bowlby stresses the ability of infants to pick up on and internalise the feelings of their parents. Some theorists, such as Piantelli, state this ability may begin in the womb.

What we are constantly hearing from clients are communications of difference, or being born flawed and imperfect. 'I'm not like my brother,' as one client stated, 'I was born all wrong'. The messages infants receive in early childhood are difficult to dislodge. More so when we as a society amplify them yet more. The life experience of a person with learning disabilities is marked by a societal reluctance to accord them with the basic tenets of respect and dignity. The links between disability and abuse are clearly rooted in the powerlessness of people with learning disabilities.

Powerlessness may be seen in the lack of protection afforded to people with learning disabilities. We wish to protect what we value. Thus people with a low sense of value or self-worth are deemed as unworthy of self-protection. This is emphasised by the dependent relationships experienced by people with learning disabilities, whose higher support needs lead to a reliance on others. For those living with an organic intellectual deficit we find evidence of a heightened tendency to accommodate those on whom care is dependent. People with learning disabilities are often described in dismissive and patronising terms which stress their 'willingness to please' and their ability 'to smile all the time'. Small wonder that these communications of passivity and compliance exist. What accompanies such ingratiation is a repression of any 'negative' emotions. What we are seeing is often a complete distortion of the true emotional state of the person. There are many other examples of powerlessness that render a person with learning disabilities more vulnerable not only to sexual abuse (i.e. poor verbal communication skills, lack of sexual education, increased access to abusers and inherent power differences exhibited most starkly in abusive residential, day-care or familial settings) but also to internalising a sense of themselves as damaged, bad and unlovable.

What we find ourselves working with is a person with an unshakable internal belief system that they have been born damaged. If this internal powerlessness then results in the experience of a sexual abuse it is often difficult for survivors to separate the original damaged goods syndrome from the secondary syndrome which is then in place. The secondary syndrome, the feeling of damage and violation born from the sexual abuse has much in common with the primary syndrome. The two syndromes become entwined in a way which is most vividly demonstrated by the words of one survivor of a vicious sexual assault: 'He put his thing in me because I'm bad'. It is important in terms of clinical work or day-to-day support on a learning disabled survivor of sexual abuse to understand that damaged goods syndrome is multi-faceted. We are not merely working with the effects of sexual trauma, we may also find ourselves working with the original trauma of being born differently.

Guilt

Guilt is a core issue which may be communicated to those around the survivor by states of depression, self-loathing, or an apparent inability to disclose their abuse without any attendant feelings of appropriate anger towards the abuser. Once more it is important to look at the damaged goods syndrome we have previously identified and separate from it the roots of guilt. It is often a core belief held within the survivor of sexual abuse that they are to blame for the abuse. This is not exclusive to survivors who have learning disabilities, but should be viewed as especially problematic when it becomes enmeshed in the client's previously held belief that they are to blame for all that has occurred in their life – starting with their birth. We return once more to the experience of being born with a disability and the pressures this imposes on the ability for self-esteem to grow. It may be useful to consider what effects there might be upon a child who receives conscious or unconscious messages that they, because of their disability, may be to blame for the extra pressures on their parents' marriage, financial problems which may have arisen, or the family's inability to enjoy healthy and uncomplicated holidays together.

Guilt is also present due to the abuse itself. Sexual abuse displaces conventional reactions. The psyche attempts to cope with the immense trauma resulting from an act of abuse. Many of its ways of coping appear erroneous. One of these is the fact that many survivors of abuse feel that they are to blame. They may have been told by the abuser, for example, that they are being abused because they have done something wrong, as in the case of the survivor who was told by his or her abusing key worker that he or she was being raped for not eating their breakfast quickly enough to get to the day centre on time.

Guilt may be one of the key reasons for non-disclosure of sexual abuse, and we must consider the immense effect it will then have upon the survivor's ability to move towards recovery and healing. As has been described in the preceding chapters, a vital role of the advocate to play is that of believer; someone who can bear to believe that the survivor's guilt is misplaced, that the act of abuse was not his or her fault, that the guilt belongs elsewhere. Unless these steps are taken the roots of guilt will remain entrapped in the survivor. This will lead to further repression and probable breakdown.

Fear

When examining the behaviours present in many learning disabled survivors of sexual abuse it is important to underpin them with an acknowledgement of the existence of fear. Fear is an intensely powerful emotion which will nurture and enlarge the nightmares and disturbed sleep patterns we may be presented with. The experience of being sexually abused will carry with it a complex set of losses. One of these will be the loss of emotional security and the failure of the survivor to feel that his or her inner or outer world is a safe place to be. Fear is most explicitly demonstrated in behaviours such as panic attacks, extreme phobias such as agoraphobia or claustrophobia or aversion to anyone resembling the abuser, whether in terms of gender or in some subtler, less tangible way. When fear is not recognised as a communication of trauma it becomes more disabling than the presence of learning disability itself. Therapeutic relationships of any kinds, whether they are conducted in the clinical setting or are simply two friends caring for each other, must contain the potential for healthy change. This change is impossible if the survivor is paralysed by their dread.

The situation is yet more difficult if the fear has been introduced by the abuser as an element of the survivor's trauma. Our clients have talked about being told that should they disclose they will have their parents killed, or they will lose their group home. It is difficult to rationalise these threats while still paralysed by the anxiety itself. For movement to occur the fear must be acknowledged in its own right as a consequence of abuse which, once addressed, will enable other presenting behaviours to be worked with. As with all of the core issues, it is a deeply internalised one which must be externalised and made sense of for the survivor.

Self-Harm

The preceding chapter alerted us to the prevalence of self-harm as a possible indicator of sexual abuse. Self-harm and self-injurious behaviour will often continue to be a core issue within the clinical setting. One of the basic tenets of our work is the acknowledgement of past horrors. In telling such a horror story a wide range of emotions will be unleashed. Some will be almost unbearable and will trigger suicidal impulses. Some will trigger memories of previously undisclosed suicide attempts. A client we shall call 'William' was referred to Respond because of his history of sexual abuse within a large hospital in which he had lived for 23 years. William had disclosed this history to the cook in his new group home, who had recognised his need to tell his story to someone else. William demonstrated a lack of emotional attachment to the horrific and disturbing story he recounted. Even when discussing the numerous occasions in which he had tried to jump off bridges or overdose on his medication William retained a toneless, passionless voice. His therapist wondered where the anger had gone. It had been 10 years since his last suicide attempt – an attempt which had resulted in a decade of antidepressant medication. In one session William described standing by a window in his group home during a violent storm. Once again this was recounted with a lack of apparent emotion. Only when the therapist inquired what feelings were going through William as he stood there did he state 'I was waiting for the lightning to strike me.' For William this was a catalyst in his therapeutic process. His rage and anger at his abuses had not been lost or medicated into oblivion. It was still an ongoing factor in his life.

There are other clients whose self-harm exhibits itself in more explicit ways – body slashing, head banging or running in front of buses. A painful reminder of the need to be aware of the potential to self-harm may be found in the case of one young man who spent 6 months of his therapy stating that he had no real need for therapy anymore, he had gotten over his father raping him and was enjoying his new work placement. While stating this, however, he continued to pick ferociously at an exposed wound on the palm of his hand, seemingly oblivious to the blood seeping from it. In this particular transference it was the therapist who was literally feeling the pain on behalf of his client.

Depression

Depression is a much overlooked consequence of the sexual abuse of people with learning disabilities. As with the preceding core issues, it may be communicated through a wide array of behaviours which effectively mask its presence. This is especially true of people with learning disabilities who often find the professionals working with them unwilling to make a diagnosis such as clinical depression. If we examine the behaviours which are associated with depression we find manifestations such as mood changes, extreme lethargy, sleep disturbances, changes in eating patterns, absence of overt emotional reactions and lack of motivation. It may be helpful to view depression as anger at the abuse turned back on the survivor and all of the preceding presenting issues as manifestations of this anger. This should be viewed once more as an example of the psyche misplacing emotional reactions. We will move on later in this chapter to examine the separate role of anger itself.

When examining the life experiences of our clients, there is a striking presence of large, institutionalised residential settings in which· manifestations of depressions have all too often been overlooked, ignored or diagnosed wrongly as simply being part of someone's character or demeanour. The sheer size of a residential setting may preclude any ability to examine the presence of clinical depression as a core issue in the lives of survivors of sexual abuse. In smaller residential settings, too, we find a surprising ability for depression within clients not to be attributed to any history of sexual abuse, but rather to be attributed to the learning disability itself. Once again we return to the societal view of people with learning disabilities as being unworthy of the same rigorousness with which we would examine non-learning disabled clients' emotional lives.

The appalling history of societal treatment of people with learning disabilities has resulted in the continuing ability for self-neglect and self-injuring to be viewed as 'part of the culture'. How vital it is for us to separate manifestations of depression from nebulously defined manifestations of living with a learning disability.

Low self-esteem

A life which is depressed, lived in fear and controlled by guilt will undoubtedly result in the core issue of low self-esteem. Figure 5.1 lists the numerous attacks on the self-esteem of people with learning disabilities. It is a worrying list, quite apart from the absent issue of sexual abuse. Many of the factors attacking the self-esteem of those we work with are political ones, such as low priority of provision funding which have resulted in such issues as sets of transitory relationships, absence of confidential listeners and stigmatism by society. All these may be seen as cumulative erosions resulting in often appalling violations of human rights. We work with clients who experience some of their most private and intimate moments with complete strangers: being helped to dress and undress. Being helped to bathe. Facing the frightening thought of saying 'good-night' to one agency member of staff in the evening and being woken by a complete stranger in the morning. This cumulative erosion of self-esteem allies itself with the previously outlined factors of powerlessness and exposed vulnerability. Where there are so many smaller, every-day abuses there is the potential for a wider set of abuses.

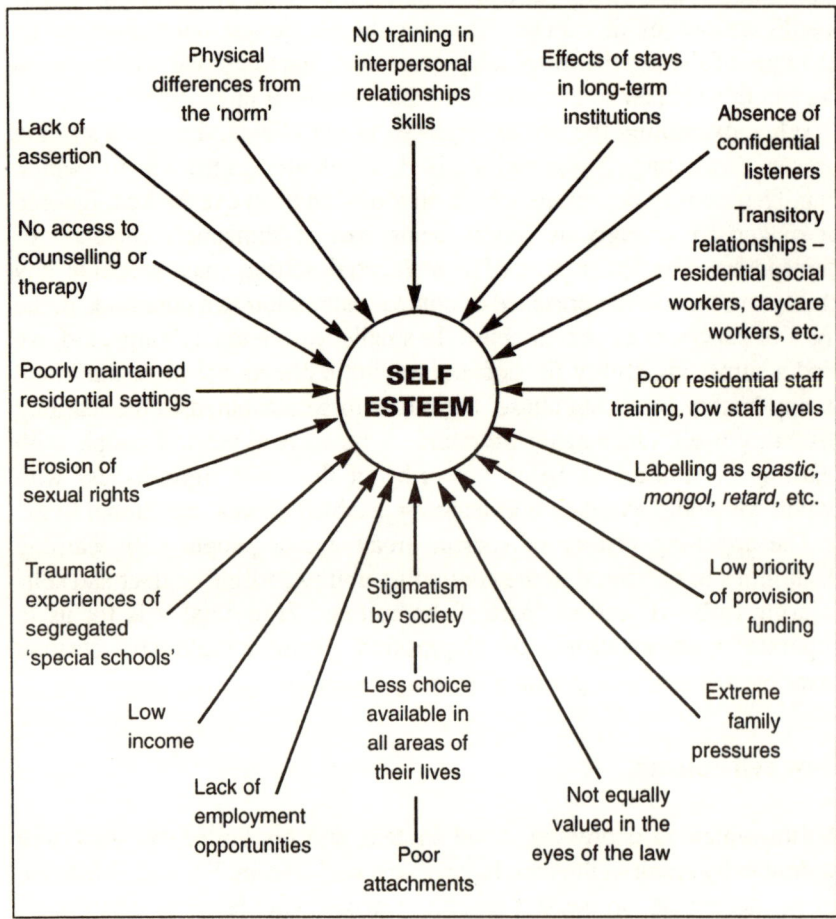

Figure 5.1 Attacks on self-esteem in the lives of people with learning difficulties

It is important to set these established attacks upon self-esteem against the wounding attack contained within the act of sexual abuse. It is difficult indeed to conceive of how the human spirit manages to survive this double set of attacks. In the cases we are working with, somehow survival has occurred, but at a cost. Loneliness and isolation are factors in many of our clients' lives, even when sexual abuse has not taken place. To encourage recovery from trauma this core issue must be recognised and acknowledged. The work of Respond was born from the ability to recognise the lack of self-esteem in the lives of our clients. It continues to be a core issue with which it is essential to work. For clients to process the trauma they have endured they must be supported in feeling good about themselves. There are many practical methods for facilitating self-esteem, from the creative and complex ones found in the plethora of self-esteem manuals available to the equally vital but often overlooked simple methods such as viewing our clients as full and valued human beings, and feeling able to see beyond the presence of disability to the human spirit that lies there.

Anger and Hostility

We have previously outlined the role of depression and its ability to be viewed as a manifestation of anger. Anger and hostility are themselves core issues which too often get split off from the person expressing the anger and the original trauma feeding it. It is important to stress the positive role anger has to play, and much of the therapeutic work Respond does engages in attempts to locate the anger that may have been repressed for years and learn ways of channelling it along healthier lines. Anger is often well hidden, either within someone's defence systems, or by other professionals, through the use of behaviour modification or the use of medication.

Anger directed inwardly has its roots in the experience of abuse and the need to kill the self rather than the abuser. 'I was bad, I shouldn't have let him do it' as one client declared, indicating his underlying guilt and the anger that had manifested itself in his frequent suicide attempts. He had returned to his all-pervading damaged goods syndrome and translated the rage underpinning it into an attempt to undo what he perceived as the cause of all his problems – himself.

In the therapeutic setting much of the anger becomes directed at the therapist. This may be due to one of a whole set of reasons. Perhaps it is simply that the survivor's anger is overflowing and the therapist is the nearest to hand. Perhaps the therapist is reminding the survivor too painfully of the abuse itself. Perhaps the therapist is reminding the survivor of the abuser. Whatever the reason, what is vital is that there is recognition of the anger as being linked to the trauma of abuse. One should never dismiss anger towards a seemingly inappropriate person as being in some way wrong, or a mistake the client is making. This extends to beyond the confines of the consulting room, to the client who suddenly gets violent towards her favourite key worker, or is found strangling her pet kitten.

The basic assumption must be made by those supporting survivors that if they have been sexually abused they will be angry. If anger does not have a place to go, it becomes distorted, repressed and dangerous. Anger is often fed by ambivalent feelings towards the abuser. The need for some form of attachment (no matter how chaotic, how abusive) become infused with rage and anger when the abuse ends, through external curtailment or through a decision made by the abuser. A woman who had been abused over a 5-year period by her mother's boyfriend appeared throughout her therapy sessions consumed with anger at her social worker for ending the relationship. 'I'll kill her next time I see her' she repeated. Towards her abuser she felt a tremendous feeling of loss, and a wish to return to the parts of the abuse that she retrospectively defined as being full of good touch, dependency and healthy attachment.

Anger should also be viewed as an essential backbone of the healing process without which therapeutic change may be difficult to attain. In the following chapter we will focus on the expression of anger as part of the mourning cycle, and examine more deeply its pivotal role in the therapeutic process. Before that it is vital to acknowledge it as a core issue in any intervention with survivors of abuse.

Inability to trust

Another loss incurred in the act of sexual abuse is the loss of trust. A client referred to Respond following a disclosure of long-term abuse by a neighbour presented a bewildering set of reactions to entering therapy. His first reaction was that he was in the consulting room to have sex with his therapist. Issues such as confidentiality became charged for him with a need to test out his therapist through strong statements of distrust. He refused to believe that anything spoken about in our sessions would be confidential, and communicated a belief that as soon as he had left the building I would be on the telephone to his social worker telling her all that we had spoken about.

The inability to trust extends into attachment terms. As we have seen, sexual abuse may often fill a need for attachment which, once it is broken, appears incapable of being replaced by anyone, be they therapist, key worker, day care manager, etc. The one person in the client's life who acknowledged them as a human being, who distorted the relationship to appear empowering, equal and loving is now revealed as someone who was either taken away or someone who chose to abuse that attachment. Small wonder that the new belief system adopted by survivors tells them never to allow anyone to adopt that attachment role.

The abuse will have involved a bodily abuse too, and for many of our clients that will have resulted in a deeply internalised conception of their body as violated beyond repair. A Respond client entered all of her early sessions almost on tiptoe, hardly daring to raise her head to engage in eye contact with her therapist. The counter-transference experienced by her therapist evoked a set of feelings of being in some way an abuser of the woman by simply being in a room with her. She sat hunched in her chair, dressed in baggy, loose-fitting clothes with barely an inch of skin exposed. Her experience of abuse had left her with a bodily association with violation and lack of control. Only once this was acknowledged as a core issue could therapeutic progress ensue.

Lowered boundaries

The most challenging clients in any service are usually those whose experience of sexual abuse has led their own sexual boundaries to become unfocused. This has impacted on their psychosexual development and ability to engage in non-abusive relationships with others. It is important to stress that most survivors of sexual abuse do not go on to sexually abuse others. The vast majority of clients engaged in therapeutic work at Respond who abuse others have, however, themselves been sexually abused.

'James' was a 35-year-old client who had been abused as a boy by a male member of staff who had entrapped him in the day centre toilets and abused him orally and anally. James's adolescence and early adulthood were marked by a series of abuses of other adolescents with learning disabilities, all of which occurred in the toilet. These sexual behaviours worsened in content until he was arrested on a charge of indecent assault. James's own survivor experience had never been addressed, therapeutically or otherwise. He had not, in fact, ever found a space in which to tell his story and so had remained frozen in the centre of it. His therapy revealed a man struggling with a deep-seated desire to remove himself from the trauma he had suffered. The only way in which this could happen was by his enacting the abuse on others. Only this time he was not experiencing the trauma as the survivor, he was experiencing it from a position of triumph. The only way in which he could regain power over his abuse was by literally becoming the victimiser.

This is undoubtedly a contentious issue, not only in the field of learning disabilities but also in the field of sexual offending, and it would be wrong to offer such a brief and simplified case study as evidence of the ability for the experience of being abused to turn into the experience of abusing. The roots of sexual offending are complex and best examined in depth in another forum. What is essential to examine here is the role of lowered sexual boundaries as a possible consequence of abuse and, as with all the preceding core issues, to retain the ability to explore below the surface of what may appear to be a superficial 'sexual acting out' and acknowledge its roots in trauma.

The lowering of sexual boundaries may also result in the survivor of sexual abuse falling into the role of sexual survivor in subsequent relationships. The link with this core issue may be found in the earlier issue of low self-esteem. We return once more to the basic violation of the sense of self inherent in a sexual attack. We have found that this can often result in the survivor of abuse repeating their role of survivor in other situations.

A client I shall call 'Janet' was referred to Respond because of child protection issues concerning her three children. Her role as a prostitute had alerted social workers to the dangers surrounding her children, all of whom were often left for long periods without her. She had recently disclosed long-term sexual abuse from her stepfather, which had led to her referral for psychotherapy. In relating her life history she spoke movingly of a series of short-term, casual relationships with men who had invariably ended up abusing her physically, emotionally and sexually. The lack of constructive support for her learning disability had driven her to view prostitution as the only viable form of employment open to her. She spoke of feeling that part of her had always been dead: 'The bit my stepdad killed', she said, 'that's been dead since then'.

Janet's story demonstrates the inability of those around her to view her lowered sexual boundaries as a result of the trauma of sexual abuse. Instead she had found herself at the receiving end of punitive, judgemental service response which viewed her sexual behaviour as something inherently 'bad' and 'uncontrollable' about her, rather than as something which needed working with therapeutically as much as her lowered self-esteem and clinical depression. The tendency to over-sexualise future relationships following abuse should be seen as a core issue in need of a therapeutic response.

Role Confusion

The blurring of sexual boundaries through the trauma of sexual abuse may also result for some clients in role and gender confusion. We have already seen the potential within sexual abuse for evoking strong phobic reactions. These may also be manifest to a greater degree in the experiences of some of our clients who have disclosed feelings of anxiety about their self-perception of their gender. A client has discussed worrying that his experience of being raped by a male member of staff would result in (his own words) 'me becoming more like a woman, or like my mum'. Instances of cross-dressing and transvestism may thus be viewed as points on the continuum of responses to sexual abuse. Within the non-learning disabled population there is a clear stigma attached to acknowledgement of the problems of such survivors of abuse. Within the learning disabled population the stigma most often graduates to extreme fear and derision – reactions allied to the societal denial of the sexual needs of people with learning disabilities.

A common fear voiced particularly by male survivors of sexual abuse is that they will adopt an exclusively homosexual orientation as a result of their abuse. There is no empirical research available to substantiate this concept. For survivors who have learning disabilities the lack of respect accorded to their right to any kind of sexuality imposes an additional trauma upon any homosexual desires which may be experienced. This lack of respect accorded towards homosexuality results in a large number of men with learning disabilities identifying public toilets as the only location in which their sexual needs may be met. Situations have also arisen for some of our clients in which their attempts at forming consensual sexual relationships with other men with learning disabilities have been defined as 'inappropriate sexual behaviour', a reaction which strips them of basic human rights and renders them yet more vulnerable to abuse in those locations where they may then be forced to go for sexual gratification.

Developmental Delay

The developmental milestones used with infants, children and young adults without learning disabilities become more difficult to adopt when a learning disability is in place. For this reason barriers to development following the trauma of sexual abuse may get ignored, minimised or wrongly defined. The ability of psychotherapy to address developmental delays following abuse indicates the error of defining a client's cognitive or functioning abilities as being fixed. The presence of sexual trauma can result in our clients becoming fixed at a certain developmental point. In the case of a client I shall call 'Andrew' his reluctance to grow beyond the age of 5 results from 5 being viewed by him as the age of innocence before he entered a special boarding school in which he was habitually sexually abused. Only within the confines of the consulting room could Andrew begin to process the trauma he had been through and as a result begin to grow.

The psychotherapist, Valerie Sinason, describes similar abilities in her abused and learning disabled client group. Both Sinason and Respond share the belief that sexual trauma can paralyse clients at a particular developmental point from which it feels unsafe, without adequate support, to emerge. Once the support is there in the form of a therapeutic alliance, or a safe and caring relationship with a concerned professional carer or family member, we may witness a gradual progress in the client's cognitive and functioning abilities.

Sex Education

Underpinning much of the above has been an acknowledgement of a societal denial of the rights of people with learning disabilities to a validation of their sexual rights. In few places is this more obvious than the paucity of sex education to this client group. The phrase 'Knowledge is power' comes to mind when considering the lack of knowledge accorded to our powerless clients. While not a core issue, the role of sex education is central to any consideration of the ongoing therapeutic support offered to a learning disabled survivor of sexual abuse. Sexual abuse may result in a deep-seated confusion in the survivor's mind. The questions of the role of sex, the ability to process sexual information and the dilemmas of dealing with sexual desires when they are shrouded in shame, guilt and fear resonate within the survivor's mind, rendering any subsequent attempt at sex education as being fundamentally flawed if it does not address the original experience of trauma.

To achieve this it is necessary to acknowledge the power of sexual information. Where there has been sexual abuse that information may automatically be equated by the survivor with the original trauma. Thus they will be unable to retain any information they receive. It will become overlaid with any combination of the core issues already described. A large number of referrals to Respond originate from a desire to provide a client with sex education. One client, whom I shall call 'Jack', was ejected from a succession of sex education groups because of what was termed his 'destructiveness' within them. When line drawings of naked bodies were shown to the group, Jack's reactions would be either to scream with fear, or to laugh hysterically at them, making it impossible for the group to continue. Sex education was seen by his staff team as vital, however, for he had a history of inappropriate sexual touch of other clients. It had been judged that the root cause of this inappropriate behaviour was his inability to retain sexual information. The question that had not been asked concerned the origins of this inability to retain information. It was only once he entered a therapeutic relationship that Jack began to disclose his own childhood sexual abuse. 'All those pictures of people with no clothes on scare me', he stated. 'They make me feel frightened all over again'.

Thus the decision to provide sex education carries with it a responsibility to ensure the education is delivered in a manner which is respectful of any possible experience of sexual abuse. Additionally it is important that the underlying trauma surrounding the client's birth should be seen as being re-evoked by any in-depth explorations of sexuality and reproduction. For clients who unconsciously view their birth as something horrific and destructive, the trauma of exploring the birth of 'normality' may be too much to bear.

HIV and AIDS

Another issue presented in Respond psychotherapy sessions is that of HIV and AIDS. It is true to say that in the early stages of Respond's therapeutic work HIV and AIDS were often cited as the main reasons for referral. A client I shall call 'Tony' entered his first therapeutic session with a list of issues written by his staff team. He himself had been a survivor of organised abuse within a day centre. The list of issues his staff team wished him to work with contained no mention of his experience of abuse. High on the list was the question of his having an HIV test. Below this were several requests for advice on safer sex practices.

It became clear that while Tony was aware of his staff team's dilemmas over whether he was HIV positive or negative, his need was to tell his story of having been abused. He would pepper his sessions with questions about whether or not he should attend a clinic for a test, but would never be able to focus on any answer his therapist might give. The notion of Tony possessing the ability to exercise informed consent was riddled with uncertainty, and remained so while he continued to struggle to disclose the whole story of his abuse. Chapter 8 looks in greater depth at the issue of staff support, although it is worth noting in the context of this case that the need for external support to enable the staff team to separate their own agenda from Tony's was paramount. Tony's therapeutic work went on to illustrate the pairing of his anxieties concerning an HIV test with his own damaged goods syndrome. The concept of him acquiring a life-threatening virus from his abuser appeared locked inside his greater anxieties about being born disabled, 'wrong', and 'abnormal', as Tony put it.

Substance Abuse

A further common theme to be found in Respond's work with survivors of sexual abuse is substance abuse, whether it be alcohol or drugs. In common with the prevalence of eating disorders such as anorexia nervosa and bulimia, substance abuse remains a common self-abusive reaction to the trauma of sexual abuse. The need, in substance abuse, to create a new inner world removed from the traumatic memories of earlier abuse, can continue for long periods and become so ingrained in the coping mechanisms of survivors that it soon becomes seen as yet another problem area of their life that is often treated in a manner that is denying of the original trauma feeding the self-abusive behaviour. The ability of alcohol or drugs to create a temporary refuge from overwhelmingly painful memories creates an unhealthy dependency which remains in place while the original trauma continues to go unheard.

Eating Disorders

In any attempt to list the huge amount of non-verbal communications attempted by learning disabled survivors of sexual abuse, the use of food continually appears. The use of food to distort the body image, to either starve or bloat, has its roots in a sense of self-esteem already starved by original trauma. It should also be seen to be linked with the issue of powerlessness previously described. For the majority of the clients we work with, the lack of external power or control over their lives is striking. In a world where power resides in others' control, small wonder that symbols of sustenance and nutrition become such powerful tools in themselves. A dangerous consequence of this is that the link between food abuse and sexual abuse will often not be made, with the result that subsequent attempts to address food issues (enforced feeding or dieting) become internalised by the survivor as re-enactments of the original sexual trauma they suffered.

Use of Bodily Waste

A final issue to explore is the use of bodily excreta as another powerful communication of trauma. A case that illustrates the ability of this difficult and taboo area to disable the carers of a survivor of abuse is that of a client we will call 'Sally'. Sally had experienced sexual abuse within her family and by members of her staff team from an early age. Much of the abuse contained ritualised elements which had begun to be disclosed by Sally in the form of drawings and pictures. Gradually she began to attach words to her pictures, and seemed to be progressing well along her therapeutic path. Prompted by the loss of a much-valued key worker, Sally suddenly appeared to go downhill. She lost interest in the drawings which had seemed to be such a key to her recovery, and began to smear her faeces over the walls of her bedroom and on occasions over herself. She refused to attend her therapy sessions, a decision accorded respect by her therapist and her staff team who recognised Sally's intelligent ability to protect herself from memories of trauma which were too painful for her to bear. It was imperative, given the break in her therapy sessions, that the communication she was struggling to make through the smearing of her faeces was recognised. The therapeutic alliance had proved too painful at that moment in her development, yet her story still needed to be told, and she was employing the most primal tools with which to tell it. We have seen the need to be an advocate both inside and out of the consulting room. The role of advocate will often be a lonely role to adopt in cases such as Sally's where one is required to translate the use of bodily waste into something meaningful. The skills of Sally's staff team was demonstrated by their being able to bear the unbearable – 'Perhaps your shit is the only thing you've got left to tell us how shitty your life has been'. It was crucial to be able to focus not only on the presenting behaviour, but the deeper communication beneath.

The core issues outlined in this chapter by no means constitute an exhaustive list. There are many more, and we will continue to learn about those new ones every time we are in a consulting room with one of our clients. What is vital in dealing with these core issues is an ability to recognise that there are few short-term ways of working with them. The experience of sexual trauma re-evokes an earlier, primal trauma which we have found to be present in the unconscious of all the clients described here, and it is vital to carry this awareness with you when embarking on any therapeutic journey with a survivor of sexual abuse who has learning disabilities.

CHAPTER 6

Three Clinical Examples

This chapter provides three examples of clients using weekly psychotherapy to recover from their experiences of sexual trauma. The names and identities of the clients have been changed together with some of the factual information in order to maintain confidentiality. In each example the psychotherapist is making use of the advocate roles as described earlier in the book. Once a referral is accepted by the therapist arrangements are made for the client to begin a period of assessment. The purpose of the assessment is to find out if the client is both suitable and ready for treatment. The process will involve 12 weekly 50 minute appointments during which the therapist will discover if it is the client's wish to make use of therapy, the nature and symptomatology of the trauma and the capacity of the client to make an emotional attachment with the therapist. Attention will also be given to the practical arrangements for any ongoing treatment including: frequency of sessions, the expected duration of the treatment, conditions of confidentiality and the consideration of any presenting special needs.

The examples provided in this chapter are representative of clients who have a developed, comprehensive vocabulary. However, there are many clients who use psychotherapy successfully without using language as their prime source of communication. The main focus of good psychotherapy is the unconscious communication which is more often than not expressed in emotion and in the counter-transference. The learning disabled client may not have access to language or sophisticated expression that is dependent on cognitive ability but this does not mean that the full range of human emotion and experience is not available.

Also represented in the following examples are the key re-occurring themes of abandonment, rejection and emotional and environmental deprivations.

Tim

The first example is from my work with a young man I will call Tim. Tim had experienced rejection and abandonment from the moment he was born. Indeed experiences of abandonment and rejection continued to be central throughout his life and clearly paved the way to him experiencing appalling abuse at the hands of a paedophile ring. Tim's early rejection was made chillingly clear to me when his mother rang the office; she was concerned that if Tim missed any of his sessions he would not get his criminal injury compensation, she had phoned the consulting rooms to check on his attendance. Following her enquiry she began to complain and she said 'I didn't want him even when he was inside me, when he came out and was mental that was even worse, he should never have been born, I didn't want him then and I don't want him now.'

Tim was referred for weekly psychotherapy because he was concerned about his increasing substance abuse. He used glue, lighter fuel and also used dope, ecstasy and alcohol. However, it was not his addictions he talked about. Tim was painfully aware of his experience of pre-birth abandonment: 'My mum didn't want me even before I was born'. His only way of coping with this realisation was to laugh every time I inquired into his relationship with his mother. He would laugh and stare silently into space as if he too was amazed at the extent of his abandonment – or indeed at what could be said.

Tim was strikingly good looking but his self-neglect was also apparent. He would arrive dressed in expensive fashionable clothes, but they would not have been washed for many weeks. He was often infested with lice and fleas. This upset him greatly but he was reluctant to do anything to change it. His dirty clothes and infestations were, however, the result of a more recent experience of abandonment. He had been thrown out of a voluntary sector residential unit because of his use of drugs. This resulted in him living in bed and breakfast accommodation, sleeping rough or using a homeless persons' refuge.

Tim attended his sessions despite the apparent lack of structure and resources in his life. During his fourth session he started to talk about his experiences of sexual abuse. At the age of 8 he was recruited into a local paedophile ring, operating on the council estate where he was living at the time. Nine men orally and anally abused Tim and a friend of his for several years. Photographs were taken of Tim dressed as a little girl taking part in various sexual acts. The photographs were used later as a bribe to keep the two boys silent. A police investigation lead to the demise of that particular ring and the perpetrators received custodial sentences. Following the trial Tim's mother sent Tim to live in Germany with his grandmother: 'I sent him to Germany, I couldn't have him in the house after the things that he had done'. Tim was later to be brought back from Germany by one of the original perpetrators who on release from jail flew to Germany and traced Tim's whereabouts. On his return Tim became involved in the 'rent boy' scene working as a prostitute and for a time lived with the man who had committed the original abuses against him.

Tim's experience of abandonment was an abandonment due to inadequacy. His mother who even before she gave birth felt inadequate to cope with a baby who would require her love and nurturing. Her inadequacy when faced with his learning disability and her inadequacy when faced with the terrible abuses he experienced all rendered her useless and unavailable for Tim. The inadequate Gran who could not offer protection. The inadequate men who perpetrated their inadequacy within the paedophile ring and the inadequate services that abandoned Tim because they could not understand his desperate coping mechanisms in relation to his inner pain – all contributed to Tim's total experience of abandonment. Tim also internalised this inadequacy and abandoned himself to inadequate coping mechanisms. His substance abuse could only numb his internal pain, it could not remove it. His attempts to provide for himself by earning money as a prostitute were also inadequate: not only did it not provide him with money, it repeatedly re-traumatised him because of the inherent sexually abusive nature of prostitution. Despite the inadequate nature of these coping mechanisms Tim had not abandoned himself. He had a sense of himself and a resilient strength.

Faced with such inadequacy abandonment Tim required a nurturing response that needed to be adequate enough to reach his pain. He required an advocate nurturer who would be there for him. In the role of nurturer I needed to let him know that I was there for him, that I could bear his pain without using or rejecting him. Tim also had needs which required practical nurturing, he required warmth, comfort and the opportunity to enjoy being clean and dry.

Psychotherapy for Tim provided a nurturing experience. Throughout the sessions Tim attended I was able to assess his movement within the survivors process as fluctuating between searching and realisation. He was not numb to the awfulness of his experiences, he was experiencing feelings to the point of physical sickness. There was, however, an all-consuming passivity which only occasionally gave way to a self-mocking laughter at his plight and never revealed the anger or rage appropriate to his situation. Tim's searching I believe was energised by an unconscious longing for a secure attachment, an attachment that would not result in abuse or abandonment. Tim was brave enough not to idealise his abusers and those who had abandoned him, but his damaged and impoverished self-esteem handicapped his sense of self. Full realisation would involve painful recognition of his learning difficulty and a knowing of how this too had contributed to his rejection and vulnerability. A secure attachment for Tim could indeed help him heal from the trauma of abuse. It would not, could not heal his handicap. For the non-learning disabled survivor of sexual abuse the process of realisation leads to an increased self-esteem and gradual internalisation of self-trust and positive identity. For Tim extending his realisation beyond the abuse would mean confronting the pain and reality of his learning difficulty. Here Tim could not be brave and reverted to creating a fantasy state induced by substance abuse in an attempt to hold back yet another terror.

In the analytic process it was important for me to recognise the presence of this further trauma facing Tim and his inability to articulate his terror, especially when such terror is presented in a variety of behaviours that disguise the reason for its presence. Mood swings, nightmares, intrusive images were all useful symbolisations that encoded the real communication that Tim was unable to express in words. As therapist, however, I was required to be brave and to find the words for him. Being a present and empathic nurturer I was able to relieve the devastating impact of speaking the unspoken. For many sessions we engaged in sensitive and delicate communication. I thought of it at the time as trying to communicate in a bubble, neither of us wanted the bubble to burst; it would have been devastating. Through interpretation, association and using the transferences I was able to speak about the reality of Tim's handicap and he, recognising that there was no risk of abandonment, was eventually able to complete a full realisation to the extent that some benefits became apparent. His nightmares ceased, he found permanent accommodation, stopped using ecstasy and alcohol and began attending a day service for young people. Tim was eventually awarded several thousand pounds in compensation for the abuses he had suffered.

Tim terminated his therapy without warning. I would like to think that his moving on was a reflection of integration, I do not know. I felt abandoned by Tim and even all these months later find myself wondering about him. My experience of abandonment is a powerful reminder that we all have need of an advocate nurturer which practically I was able to find within supervision and through the support of colleagues.

Jenny

The next example concerns a 22-year-old woman, Jenny. Jenny required an advocate protester. Someone who would protest on her behalf and work to release her own silenced voice of protest. Jenny also had experienced abandonment: she was abandoned to a tyranny. The tyranny of her family and her father. Their oppression of her consisted of emotional, physical and sexual abuse which only ceased when I instigated a legal intervention. Incidents of emotional abuse, however, still occur.

Jenny was referred by her new social worker who had been able to witness what Jenny was saying. The social worker without recognising it was in fact utilising the role of advocate witness and was not only able to hear, she was also able to believe and recognise the tyranny for what it was. However, Jenny's experience prior to this had indeed been different and had caused her to become mad on a number of occasions.

During a period of 5 years Jenny had told others whom she believed could help her, that she was being sexually abused by her father. She told a day centre worker 'My father is doing horrible things to me, he puts his private part into me.' The worker replied, 'Don't be stupid that only happens to children, you're a grown woman, your father would not do that to you'. Because this day centre worker could not bring herself to witness the truth in what Jenny was saying, because the truth was so unbearable the day centre worker also became disabled and chose not to see or witness what Jenny was clearly communicating. Jenny found herself abandoned by disbelief.

Some months later Jenny told a community worker at the local church which she attended. 'My father does horrible things to me, he does it when my mum goes out and no one believes me'. The community worker responded: 'We all get annoyed with our fathers but there's no need to say terrible things like that'. Jenny was once again abandoned by disbelief. This community worker was willing to protect the position and integrity of a father she had just been told was doing horrible things. She was able to abandon Jenny to this father who did horrible things, without raising questions. I was reminded of the maxim 'Honour thy father and mother'. The practice of this honouring is a Victorian value that is active in our society today – for some with disastrous consequences.

The consequences for Jenny were indeed disastrous. From the age of 17 her father had been forcing full sexual intercourse onto her. When mother left for an evening class each Tuesday evening Jenny would be vaginally penetrated and on occasions orally abused by him. Throughout Jenny's attempts to tell, this abuse continued unabated.

I said that Jenny became mad, and I believe her madness was a direct consequence of not being believed. Some months following yet another attempt to be believed Jenny started self-injuring and was admitted to a psychiatric hospital. When her reality was not recognised, when her experiences she knew to be real were not validated she needed to defend herself from the pain of not being believed. Jenny was able to self-injure and express herself using 'mad' defences because she had already numbed herself in an attempt to not feel the abuse she had endured. Telling was her first attempt to be brave enough to feel again. When that telling was met with disbelief and abandonment she returned to her defence. As Valerie Sinason (1992) has illustrated, madness is sometimes a most intelligent defence. Jenny's use of madness proved to be just this. Because Jenny became mad she was allocated a social worker. This social worker was able to believe Jenny and as result Jenny stopped self-injuring. The social worker at first sought the help of the specialist psychologist who unfortunately abandoned Jenny and the social worker: 'I will work with her learning difficulty but not the sexual abuse'. The outrage of this abandonment was felt acutely by Jenny who immediately started self-injuring again and when she first presented at her first session with me she had also elected to not speak.

It was important for me to state: 'I can bear your silence and I will not go away when you decide you want to speak to me about the horrible things that have happened to you'. This needed to be a constant message for several sessions. In the advocate role I needed to let Jenny know I could bear to be her witness. Whilst in the analytic process faced with her silence I was required to work on the recovery and disclosure of memories. When Jenny did begin to speak to me she first related her experiences of abandonment. For a while the experience of abandonment by others was a greater abuse which Jenny could not bear.

The first 26 sessions with Jenny were in fact disclosure sessions. Facilitating a full recovery of memory with Jenny was crucial in preventing future defences and denial. As therapist I could hold the disclosures and painful knowledge and thus prevent further repression. Jenny had arrived in therapy remembering much detail of her abusive experiences but it is worth noting that several of the first 26 sessions were silent sessions in which Jenny used her mute defence whilst I struggled with the realisation that new memories of past abuse were surfacing. These were difficult times for Jenny: nightmares and flashbacks would occur to the extent that her sleep pattern was becoming increasingly disturbed. Jenny would take a recorded visualisation and relaxation technique to bed with her and on waking from a nightmare rather than remain passive to the flashback would put the tape on her portable tape machine and replace the flashback with her positive visualisation. This was an empowering activity which Jenny could use herself to contain and hold, reinforcing the message that she could be in control of what were previously occurrences out of her control. Jenny's long process of disclosure moved her further towards integration of her traumas and enabled her to break through the defence of silence. Through Jenny's disclosures I realised the extent of the tyranny to which Jenny had been abandoned. Her family – the still-abusing father, the non-believing and non-present mother and her brothers who not only didn't believe her but also teased her – together formed a tyranny, a power greater than Jenny.

Once Jenny trusted the new secure attachment within therapy she revealed further effects of her experiences of disbelief. Jenny had become accepting of her situation. She saw no reason why the abuse should be stopped or indeed how it could be stopped. This situation required me to become the protester and to encourage further progression into the survivor's process. The protesting statements included: 'That is wrong of your father, I think it's wrong and terrible and the law thinks it's wrong and terrible', 'What a terrible way to treat you his daughter', 'Because this is wrong we can stop it' and 'I feel angry that so many people who could have helped you, chose not to believe you'. Eventually Jenny started to become angry herself. At first she would feel intense guilt and shame following the angry outbursts against her still abusing father. Following a particularly difficult session in which she revealed that her father had begun to threaten her with a knife if she did not comply to his wishes, Jenny decided that it was time to go to the police.

Joint work involving a mutual respect for the different professionals roles and skills involved is crucial for the investigative process. I was fortunate in already having a liaison with the local child protection team, and previous experience had taught me to keep extensive and precise written details of all Jenny's sessions. Jenny arrived for her investigative interview wearing a badge which stated in large letters 'Yes, no – maybe'; the significance of this was to be demonstrated later when she needed to make a decision allowing the police to proceed further. In the final stages of the investigation Jenny said she could not make up her mind; she could not let the police confront her father. 'Maybe' she said again and again. Deciding to wait until she was ready we continued weekly sessions. I would like to note here the importance of Jenny's anger. This anger was the materialisation of her inner strength. However, when someone with a learning difficulty expresses anger the response of services is usually control and repression. Expressions of anger are rarely recognised as a justifiable expression or communication, if you have a learning difficulty and express anger then you are often medicated, put on a behaviour modification programme, denied food and sometimes locked up. As Jenny's advocate protester I was able to reassure her that it was fine to be angry and that she had every reason to be angry. Jenny used her anger to move powerfully through her survival process and reminded me of its creative and healing qualities.

During this time Jenny's family became suspicious of her sessions and demanded to see me. With the abuse continuing Jenny decided that I should visit her mother with the police. The extent of denial and rage directed towards myself by Jenny's mother resulted in a violent attack. Jenny was asked to leave the family home and was once again abandoned by her mother and sisters.

Further interviews between the police and father did not result in any charges being brought. Jenny was placed in a small group home and continues to attend for weekly therapy. Father still occasionally rings Jenny to remind her of all the trouble she caused.

For many years Jenny was trapped within the powerful abusive structure of her family which I came to see as a tyranny that existed to work against her and deny her a voice. It was important for Jenny to hear an advocating protesting voice. Her madness had rendered her silent and she would need to rediscover her voice before she could protest. My voice on her behalf did not just witness what was happening to her, it protested about it and said this was wrong, it should not happen and need not continue to happen. The protesting voice was able to bring about change, and is a powerful reminder to me that the therapeutic process is not passive and can when appropriate be used for intervention.

It was not easy for me to protest. At times I was conscious that I was a lone voice against a large and powerful establishment that had made clear their refusal to believe. I recognised counter-transference as feelings of isolation and loneliness. I too experienced the abandonment of others whom I believed would be there for me, the psychologist for one.

This is a positive example of the law as a willing protester. However, I needed to be constantly aware that this relied upon my ability to stand firm in my boundaries of therapist, to respect the difference in our roles and to recognise and facilitate the working together of those roles.

Jenny's voice of protest continues to grow, she still experiences abandonments but is able to recognise that she does not need to resort to madness to cope. She can go to those who are able to confirm her reality and validate her experiences of the world.

Jenny's family were unable to accept her for what she was, and instead of living alongside Jenny and her disabilities, they fought hard against them, creating a harsh and controlling environment which became a powerful and abusive tyranny in Jenny's life. When Jenny tried to break out of her abandoned situation her would-be 'helpers' also abandoned her. People with learning difficulties have a great need for the advocate protester.

Helen

The final example concerns a women called Helen who required me to be an advocate witness, in fact an advocate witness to the unbelievable. Helen is a young women with a mild learning difficulty. She was abducted and ritually abused by a satanic coven some years ago before our ability to believe the existence of such practices had been tested. Helen – although at times functioning in a dissociated state and communicating her pain through self-injuring, suicide attempts, and alcohol abuse – was able, when faced with someone who could bear to witness, not only to tell what had happened but could also reveal that she had become accustomed to others' disbelief and their desire not to believe.

At the first session on entering the consulting room Helen said 'You will only hear half of it, there is another half but they didn't believe it then. They don't believe it now and you won't believe it either, will you?' Helen, whilst showing understanding, was searching for my ability to believe – I was able to offer Helen belief but this did not come easily. I wanted to dismiss the information that Helen gave to me as crazy, I wished her experiences could be explained by referring to fantasy, a false reality. However, my work with other survivors of abuse has taught me to pay close attention to counter-transference feelings and I was able to recognise that wishing Helen's reality was crazy was her wish too. Helen knew what she knew as reality would not go away. Her wish to go away from it was fulfilled by dissociation and, entering into a state that she described as 'like being in cotton-wool'.

Long before Helen disclosed any information about the abuse she had suffered she would arrive at sessions in her 'cotton wool' state, she would move quietly around the room, whispering and mumbling to herself and then she would start to talk about me as if I were absent: 'What shall I tell him today?' 'No not that, he won't believe that. He's shitty anyway and so fat. I don't want him to know'. This would continue for 10 minutes or so and then she would suddenly address me in a sharp manner, she would assume an Irish accent and talk to me in the fashion of a no-nonsense Dublin woman. She would mock and jib at me calling me mental and spastic. Helen was powerful in this dissociated role. It fully masked the little Helen who was so traumatised by the abuse. Helen the 'no-nonsense Dublin women' was the adult Helen trying to forget and make sense of all that had happened. I also needed to remember the Helen who was 7 and abducted, drugged, tied up and raped within a satanic circle, who still experienced the fear and horror of those moments as present-day realities.

Working with both would be essential if Helen was eventually to tell her experiences and move on into integration. However, there were complex issues to face. Helen only gave me glimpses of her vulnerable child self and remained for many months as the coping adult. Also, Helen's dissociation was not typical of the regressive state back to childhood which I know to be common with dissociated non-learning disabled clients. Helen's dissociated persona was able and articulate. Again it was a powerful reminder that Helen lived with the trauma of knowing she had experienced satanic abuse and with the knowledge that she had a learning disability. I would need to be able to contain both. Dissociation back to childhood offered Helen no comfort that would have come close to the trauma of being born 'not right', a term which she was later to use. It was easier for Helen to dissociate into a projection of herself as she wished herself to be. By doing so Helen found a way of living with double trauma.

Speaking directly to the non-learning disabled persona facilitated an outpouring of rage against having a learning difficulty and how this was the cause of all the abuses. Following several sessions that consisted of an outpouring of self-blame and immense guilt, Helen arrived at the session and told me that during a visit to her grandmother's house she had looked into an old photograph album for photographs of herself when she was younger. She explained that she was searching to see if she had been born wrong or if she had become wrong latter, after the abuse. Helen did not dissociate at this point and proceeded to ask me about the nature of her learning difficulty. I believe this exploration was due to the fact that I had willingly encouraged an alliance between her persona and myself as an aware witness. Having borne that trauma Helen was further able to use the confidence gained in our attachment. However, she was cautious and could not risk abandonment. The full disclosure of the satanist abuse was approached through a series of dreams.

The first drawings that Helen brought to her sessions I believe were dreams. They contained indications of painful repressed experiences but there was nothing indicating ritual abuse. However, by the sixth presentation the drawings of the dreams changed in quality and in content. The drawings became detailed and involved lines or circles of people watching Helen whilst horrible things occurred to her. In one dream people watched as she was killed by a car. In another dream people watched her brain being cut open and in another a circle of penis-shaped figures looked on whilst she lay dead. The final dream which Helen used to disclose the half that had not been told involved Helen laying at the bottom of a hill, dead. Going up the hill there were several penis-shaped trees. Helen explained that she had really been at the bottom of such a hill, in a graveyard, carried there by her uncle who had abducted her from the special school she had attended. Further details followed as she described the satanic ritual carried out by her uncle and several other people. Recognising Helen's use of dreams to make a chilling reality bearable for me ensured for her my presence and belief. In a most intelligent way Helen had found a way to exorcise her traumas and to place within an appropriate attachment rather than resorting to dissociation or self-harm.

It is 2 years ago that I first started struggling to be a witness for this client. At that time I dared not speak out about the fact that I was working with a survivor of ritual abuse. I feared that I would be discredited and I feared that I would not be believed. Believing that no one could bare to be a witness for me, initially I remained silent and could only bear to tell the whole story at the invitation of my supervisor.

Helen was abandoned by her family who did not, could not, recognise her vulnerability. They felt more able to trust the parenting skills of a boarding school than their own. The institution of the boarding school, however, also lacked awareness and parenting skills. It abandoned Helen to an uncle without making appropriate checks.

Helen was also abandoned by the legal system who only believed half of her story. They accepted the evidence of sexual assault but ignored any reference to the involvement of others and certainly ignored any reference to ritual elements of the abuse.

Helen was also abandoned by the perpetrators of what I now understand to be a devouring force. For Helen has been abandoned to live her life in fear, a tangible fear that is visible and powerful and at times beyond my reach. I am not inferring supernatural qualities to this force. But I understand it to be the response of the psyche to extreme degrees of torture and abuse. The fear experienced at the time of the trauma does not go away, instead it becomes integrated into daily life and and manifests itself in associated forms whenever related incidents or projections trigger an association. Helen is fearful of living and so surrounds herself with images of death and anything that threatens life: murder stories, horror videos, visiting graveyards, writing suicide notes, drawing and talking of blood and death. These fantasies and projections make her real-life experiences of horror appear bearable.

As witness I also have to bear them and let Helen know that I can. In the face of such fear I need to be confident and reassuring and constantly provide the alternative which is security and a sense of peace.

The devouring effect of involvement in satanic abuse is reflected in Helen's inability to distinguish right from wrong. Satanist's reverse completely the common good; it is wrong to murder becomes it is right to murder. The internalising of this belief is so complete for Helen that in her journal writings any references to good is spelt back to front; she is not dyslexic in any other instances.

The cost of being a witness can be high. Without adequate support and understanding from friends, colleagues, family and partners this work cannot be, and should not be done. The counter-transference issues I faced and am facing concerning Helen include fear, feelings of sickness and nausea, feelings of being contaminated and needing to shower following sessions, feelings of isolation and self-doubt. There are also practical problems specific to work with ritual satanic abuse and these concern the risk of intimidation. Silent phone calls at the office and at home, reported knowledge of your locality, and abuse within the sessions themselves. All aspects which the therapist witness must be prepared to bear.

Helen seeks to protect me from her horrors by relating them as dreams and then tells me to 'fuck off and eat my shit' when I witness the reality of her pain. At times I become her intestines and she uses the whole session to stuff me full of all that she wants me to pass out.

Helen will continue this process for some time yet and I am reminded that in the face of such a devouring force of evil, as therapist I am able and required to be a witness to that which is good and right.

CHAPTER 7

Group Work for Women

This chapter is based on the working experience of the Women's Survivors Group which has been part of Respond's work since January 1994. The group was funded for 3 years by a special project grant from the Department of Health. It has been co-facilitated by Tamsin Cottis and Janet Hughes. The chapter will explore the therapeutic work which goes on in the group and also some of the organisational issues which it has raised.

From the outset we envisaged that Respond would work with groups as well as with individuals. We felt strongly that the voice of the victim was not heard when people with learning disabilities were sexually abused. Our combined experience as groupworkers had given us a commitment to work in which people with learning disabilities could find strength through sharing emotions and feelings in a safe context. We felt this could be especially helpful when people with learning disabilities shared an experience of having been sexually abused. Many of the factors which make them vulnerable to being abused are organisational and not concerned with any organic handicap. These are, for example, having to live in the family home for longer, in staffed situations where power imbalances are part of the structure, or growing up in emotionally neglecting environments which do long-term damage to self-esteem and can lead to impoverished relationships and repressed sexuality.

In a group for survivors, members have an opportunity to recognise that they are not an individual set of problems and thereby in some way responsible for the bad things which happen to them. Many of the reasons for their abuse and the nature of the abuse itself as well as its consequences are shared by others who are labelled as having learning disabilities. A number of members of the group have been abused within their families. Pam, who is no longer allowed to see either of her parents, has learned that Sally, too, no longer has contact with her father. Sally is able to express her anger at her father very clearly and access her feelings about him. This has helped Pam – who initially described what had happened to her with a smile on her face – recognise that what she experienced was very wrong and that she has a right to feel angry about it. For the first time she can see herself as a person who was sexually abused and not as a naughty girl who deserved to be punished. The group facilitators can give this message, but it is reinforced more powerfully by the direct experience of another group member.

Setting the group up

We publicised the group through our existing networks and eight women joined the group on a 'first-come, first-served' basis. We have never preselected members as we have not wished to make prejudgments about either their capacity to participate in a group, or the severity of their abuse and its consequences. We see it as our task to be flexible and creative in finding ways of communicating with people.

The group includes members who have been abused within the family as children or young adults: others have been abused by their paid carers, by other service users or by social acquaintances: for some this abuse is recent, for others in the distant past.

Initially, we had wanted to have minimal referral procedures so that women could come to the group free of preset agendas and that our minds would be clear to hear whatever they chose to tell. We discovered, however, that we needed to foster closer relationships with referrers. One reason for this was that members became distressed by what they heard others saying in the group but felt unable to ask for support outside the group because material was confidential. Now, each potential member of the group visits the project with a referrer before she starts to attend. We make it explicit that she may need support in between group sessions and a key support figure is identified. This initial meeting makes subsequent communication with outside support networks easier. Recently there was an incident in which one member attacked another one in the group. Both parties were extremely upset by the incident, particularly the attacker. We were able to talk to the attacker's key worker and explain what had happened and also to give the strong message that she would not be punished or removed from the group because of what had happened. On another occasion we became concerned that a group member was in current danger of being sexually abused. The confidentiality policy of Respond states that we will not keep private information which indicates that a person is in danger. The policy helps keep our work safe and because we had had an opportunity to make it clear to the member and their referrer at the introductory meeting, it was much easier to follow up the allegations which were made. (As well, we regularly remind members of this policy and explain it in ways which are meaningful to them.)

The introductory meeting gives prospective members the opportunity to meet the facilitators, find out more about the group and decide if they would like to give it a try. We do not ask for lots of information about the abuse that has occurred but say: 'This is a group for women with learning disabilities who have been sexually abused, how do you think it will help you?' At this stage, some people are not able to say anything much – perhaps just that their dad treated them badly. Others will say a lot about what happened. Some may say nothing, but remain adamant that they want to come to the group. The information shared by the group member at this stage will give us an insight into how far they have gone in the process of recovery. They will indicate, for example, their current feelings towards the abuser, and who they feel is responsible for the abuse. Although we are not working to preset goals in terms of recovery, our aims are that by the end of the group the members will have a clearer sense of what has happened to them and have more access to their feelings concerning the abuse. Particularly, we hope the women will come to recognise that they were not to blame for the sexual abuse which occurred.

Content and process

The purpose of the group is that the women in it have the opportunity to share what has happened to them so that they can better understand their abuse and its consequences. Each session, each woman that wants to talk, has a chance for her own space to share what is on her mind that week. Sometimes this will be about the sexual abuse that she has experienced in the past and sometimes it will be about issues of more current concern. These tend not to be mundane or everyday things but contemporary incidents of bullying, or being misrepresented, or struggling to make their voice heard.

Each session is 2 hours long and we break for a drink after the first hour. The members use the break to talk to us on their own, or else to have a bit of space away from us, talking to each other. In the beginning the group was more structured and we as facilitators were active in planning the sessions and developing and adapting exercises which would help the group to feel safe, and make it okay to express a range of feelings in the group, including negative ones. Members were at varying stages of knowing that they had joined a group for women with learning difficulties who had been sexually abused – and there were many questions such as 'what is abuse?' and 'what is a learning difficulty?' Work on flipcharts was popular in the group and members often asked to use flipcharts as issues emerged – not everyone could read and write and yet they valued us writing down their words and keeping them safely. Knowledge can be empowering: knowledge also led the women to recognise the enormity of what had happened to them, and from the beginning much pain was shared in the group.

As the group has evolved each woman's use of her individual space has grown and other activities have become superfluous. Our capacity and the capacity of the group to stay with painful material has enabled each woman to share more and more of her story and to work at a deep level as she tries to make sense of what has happened to her. For many of the women in the group, the experience of sexual abuse has triggered painful feelings about other aspects of their emotional lives and in particular their lack of a basic sense of being loved and wanted as a child born with a disability. Whilst the facilitators have needed to take an active role in ensuring that these individual spaces are not sabotaged, the women have shown themselves able to listen and make relevant and empathic comments. For example, when one woman was describing an incident in which she had lost her temper another group member said, 'when I feel like that I go up to my room and hit my pillow' and 'I'm angry about what happened to D'.

Most of our communication is with spoken words although the members show their feelings in all sorts of ways. By crying, by shouting, by refusing to come in, by exiting to go to the toilet, by bringing gifts and cards for each other. As well, there is always an opportunity to draw. In the early days of our work together there were a number of women who found it difficult to talk, so they would draw what had happened to them and then tell us about the drawing. Sometimes the disclosure dolls in the room have been used to represent the abuser or victim and several women have written down their feelings or we have acted as scribes for them.

The therapeutic approaches employed at Respond, which have been described in earlier chapters are all in use within the women's survivors group. All in the group at different times act as witness, nurturer and protester to each other; the idea that there is an inner child inside every woman there, that needs caring for, especially if it has been hurt; and that many losses have occurred through being sexually abused which need to be mourned and worked through are ideas which guide us in our work with the group. These examples from the group will illustrate how.

Whenever a member of the group is talking about what has happened to her we will be her witnesses by taking time to listen carefully. We will acknowledge when something bad was experienced: 'That was terrible. You must have felt very frightened when your Dad threw you down on to the bed.' We will give the women a chance to tell what has happened as often as they need to. Our witnessing has allowed those abused as young children to see what happened to them more clearly. Alice talked about having to witness her mother having sex with a variety of men: 'I was little. She shouldn't have done that. I couldn't go anywhere else, it was wrong. I was little. I didn't like it.'

It is also part of our witnessing role to allow the expression of negative feelings but we have had to balance this therapeutic demand with a concern for the feelings of other group members who may be attacked or victimised. When this happens we support both parties and try to make clear what is happening. The group has rules which the members have devised for themselves and these incorporate the need to be kind and respectful towards one another.

We are aware also that a group member may start by describing something which is apparently positive – a family wedding, for example, or a forthcoming holiday. If we can stay with them as they talk and not tell them what they are feeling, this allows space for us to see the fear or sadness or anger which may lie alongside what they are saying. One member was able to talk about the powerful jealousy of her cousin who was getting married, and of her acute sadness that she would never be beautiful like her cousin

There have been occasions when the members of the group have wanted others outside to witness their experiences and some have given testimony on video – and for one woman this will be used as part of a training film.

There are many ways in which the group can act as a protester. Facilitators and other group members are protesting witnesses to the pain and injustice endured. Individually and collectively we name the guilt of the perpetrator. When a group member told us that she had been abused by a carer and we fulfilled our obligations to inform other people, she told us in the knowledge that people in the group would take the matter seriously and that it mattered she was treated badly. 'It's physical abuse, isn't it?' she kept repeating. She was worried about what would follow from her disclosure but she was strong enough to protest in this instance. Another member was being harassed by another day centre user who kept asking her to kiss him as he followed her around. She could name this as sexual harassment and as sexual abuse.

Protesting can lead to the discharge of angry feelings and the women in the group know we will not condemn them for this. Not surprisingly, a growing sense of anger at what has happened has been accompanied by sadness too, particularly in relation to the loss of family relationships. This sadness has often been expressed and although there have been times when a vulnerable member of the group has found it hard to be faced with another's vulnerability, on the whole we can respond to these expressions of sadness with empathy. This will often be expressed by other group members in their willingness to give someone who is upset time to talk without interrupting them. We try always to acknowledge the power of this listening.

The group has a very significant nurturing role and it has grown in importance as the women have revealed more of their painful past experiences and the difficulties they face in their present lives. The group members have been nurturing towards one another and are very conscious of who is absent or present. Each member's birthday is acknowledged, as are illnesses and new items of clothing, hairstyles etc. As the group has evolved the members increasingly engage in conversations at the beginning and end of sessions, as well as in the break, which are not directed by the facilitators This is an indication of growing confidence and trust amongst members.

All situations where abuse is worked with contain the vulnerable children in the survivors and we often find ourselves working with these vulnerable children. One member who is frequently overwhelmed with sadness will cry into the lap of one of the facilitators. Another member will provide her with tissues. We will not demand 'adult' behaviour and continue to assert their right to be upset and receive comfort in their distress.

The process of the group also involves dealing with the separations and reunions which are an intrinsic part of it. There is often anger at times of holidays, or someone will show that they feel rejected by rejecting us and staying away from the group for a week or two. We give plenty of notice of holiday dates and encourage members to do the same. Throughout the life of the group, people have left and new members have joined. We have tried to keep the membership as stable as possible recognising that this is important if trust and safety is to develop. This has had to be managed sensitively when vacancies have occurred and new people have joined. This happened only early on in the first two terms of years one and two and not at all in the last 9 months of the 3 years.

To summarise our role as facilitators, it is our task to model the advocate roles for group members, allowing them space to develop their abilities to do this for themselves and others. We had a responsibility to establish ground rules and ensure that they are adhered to, as part of the provision of a safe and nurturing environment. At times we have needed to protect the space of a group member or make sure they are not victimised. Supported by supervision and our own therapy, we are able to provide containment for the group and we have found that one of us cannot do this on our own. Often one of us needs to focus on a member who is disclosing, whilst the other facilitator enables the rest of the group to listen and hold on. Occasionally one of us has to go out with one member, because they need support, or because they cannot accept the ground rules. We have found that we cannot leave the women on their own during the break, as this is a time when conflict and victimisation can occur.

As the women began to work more deeply in the group our advocate translator role developed, heightening awareness of how the past effects the present and future and working with the conflict that came into the group.

Supervision and evaluation

Working with the group has been demanding for us. At the end of each session we spend up to 45 minutes talking together about what has happened in the group and sharing how we are feeling. This opportunity for mutual support and shared reflection is essential. We would also recommend that anyone embarking on work such as this has regular skilled supervision from outside. This has helped us to achieve greater insight into group processes and provided us with containment for our own feelings.

The focus of our post-session discussions will often be evidence of new thinking or self-expression from members in the group. We notice, for example, when Tina can talk about being sexually abused by her father without needing to laugh in embarrassment as she talks or when Sally has managed to listen for a long stretch of time without needing to draw attention to herself. Our weekly notes also focus on each individual, as well as on general content and process, and have proved a valuable record of change and development.

There are regular opportunities for members to express their own thoughts and feelings about the group during sessions. Sometimes this arises naturally and at other times we have actively sought their views because we are talking about the group at a meeting. They have welcomed being involved in this way, as long as their own names are not used.

At the end of each of the first two years, we talked to each member on their own about how they were finding the group and how they think it helps. At this point they were invited to decide whether to leave the group or make a commitment for a further year.

As the 3 years draw to a close, we are looking with each individual member at what they have gained from the group. This self-assessment by group members is helping them to recognise their own emotional development, and clarify their future needs.

In the course of our ongoing evaluation of the group, we began to question whether the group could meet all of the women's emerging needs. After one year of operation we felt strongly that the opportunity for individual therapy should be there for any member who required it and set about acquiring funds specifically for this purpose. As a result of this a black member has been able to enter therapy, with a black therapist, whilst continuing to attend the group and two other women chose to engage in individual therapy as a preferred alternative to the group. At the time of writing we would assert that, whilst not being essential for each member,individual therapy would be beneficial alongside the group as it would mean that each woman would know that they would have more space to talk at some time in the week and have more freedom to explore in-depth feelings. As the group has developed, everyone in it has more to say and time constraints mean that we inevitably have to intervene to make sure everyone has a turn.

In considering the place for groupwork, we found it useful to ask ourselves 'what would the group members lose if they did not have the group?'

We recognise that the group is an opportunity for:

- a sharing of painful experiences
- the acquisition of a sense that the abuse was wrong
- the validation of this injustice from others
- a strong peer experience
- a therapeutic experience which is less intimate than individual therapy. This may be especially helpful in the early stages of recovery.

Groupwork is very powerful. The effect of a concentration of emotion can propel members into expressions of feelings which may otherwise have remained buried for a long time. Whilst this needs to be recognised as a strength of groupwork, attention must also be paid to the fact that disclosure can leave people feeling exposed and vulnerable. Provision must be in place for support outside the group and sensitivity to individual needs must not get buried beneath the excitement which can be generated through collective working.

CHAPTER 8

Professional Issues

One of the aims of this book is to provide a template for good practice in work with survivors of sexual abuse who have learning disabilities. It has taken Respond many years to develop the professional support systems described within this chapter. We are aware that for many workers struggling with a suspicion of sexual abuse, a disclosure of abuse or in supporting a survivor along the road to recovery and healing the range of support structures developed by Respond may simply not exist. They must still, however, be striven for. Working with sexual abuse attacks the vulnerable part of all of us, professional or layman. Becoming a witness, protester, nurturer and translator to a survivor of sexual abuse means that we will be witness to the most appalling details of abuse, we will wish to protest against the often unbelievable acts of abuse our fellow human beings are capable of, we will struggle to nurture the tiniest fragments of a shattered sense of self, and we will attempt to translate not only words, but other arduous communications such as silences, self-injurious behaviours, sexual acting out and smearing. To progress down this difficult road without serious consideration being given to the support needs of the worker is ultimately a form of denial of the effects of sexual abuse itself – not only on the survivor of abuse but also on those attempting to support the survivor.

The recommendations we will make stem from our experience as an independent and developing psychotherapy provider. The benefits of the impartiality of our position do not negate the application of our methods of working to other agencies and services. The basic guidelines to consider in supporting survivors of sexual abuse are born out of an acknowledgement of what human beings need in order to help victims of trauma, regardless of work setting.

We will firstly focus on the practicalities of supporting a client who is in psychotherapy or counselling, drawing on our own clinical and practical experience. In commencing work with a client it has become increasingly clear to us that we also need to consider how we will work with the client's support network. There must be a clarity within the team as to the role of psychotherapy in the client's life. 'Julie', a woman we are working with, found her therapeutic process impeded by the conflicts at play within the professionals around her. A number of her care staff valued Helen's time within therapy, and communicated this through their consistency in ensuring Helen arrived at her sessions on time, that her journey to Respond was smooth and stress free, and that she was accorded the silence she clearly needed following her sessions.

The reverse was true of the remainder of her team who felt that Helen's emotional stability would be best served by allowing her quietly to forget the rape she had endured. They exhibited a resentment against the rest of the team for what they perceived as a needless weekly return to her experience of trauma. When members of this part of Helen's team were on duty we would find that she would fail to appear for her sessions without any warning, or on those occasions when she did arrive she would be forced to deal with a stream of intrusive questions as soon as she emerged from her clinical session.

The lesson to be learnt from the experience of Helen's team was that unless this form of split within a team is acknowledged and addressed Helen's ability to engage in a secure attachment with her therapist will be severely impeded. A crisis point arrived when it became clear that Helen was accessing more memories of her original abuse. She grew depressed between each session, and would spend hours crying helplessly in her bedroom. This set of reactions to loss alarmed the team who had been struggling with her use of therapy. Attempts were made to curtail her time formally at Respond. Eventually a meeting was called in which the difficulties voiced by parts of Helen's team were verbalised and addressed. Her case highlights the need for clarity on the professional issues we will now examine. If this clarity does not exist, responses to traumatised clients are in danger of becoming chaotic, inconsistent and re-traumatising.

Choice of therapeutic modality

The treatment choices available to people with learning disabilities who have been sexually abused are extremely limited, and may be dictated by a wider set of external considerations: financial, pragmatic and time-limited. We recommend that the analytic model of therapeutic work as described in the preceding chapters be accorded equal consideration alongside the more popular disciplines such as behaviourist response or a more purely cognitive model. The ability of the analytic model to work with the unconscious, to recognise the paralysing effects of loss, to use the tools of transference and counter-transference and to explore the role of secure and insecure attachments has resulted in our clients' growing ability to process the trauma they have suffered and learn to function more ably in a world already characterised for them by rejection, fear and stigmatism. Many have come to us from more behaviour-focused modalities which appear to have done little to address the underlying clinical issues they present.

Decisions will also need to be made about the preference for group or individual therapeutic intervention. We would stress the dangers of this decision focusing purely on the economic advantages of group work as opposed to individual work. Group work, as we have seen in Chapter 7 has many advantages in terms of increased relation to peers, exploration of group cohesiveness through the identification of the shared experience of sexual abuse leading to improved client motivation. Despite these factors, for many clients a group evokes an unacceptably large set of fears which will impede therapeutic progress. A combination of both group and individual work has been found to work well with particular clients, while some are in a group for some time before deciding to engage purely in individual therapy.

Introductory session

We are referring in this context to the beginning of therapeutic work with a client who has either disclosed sexual abuse or who has indicated that he or she has been sexually abused. By the point at which a client enters Respond's therapy provision we hope that the client has been given a clear idea of the concept of psychotherapy and, from this information, has been able to give informed consent to engaging in the psychotherapeutic relationship. The first sessions vary dramatically in content from client to client. With some clients it is viewed as a chance to ask questions of the therapist to begin to build a secure base from which therapeutic progress may commence. With other clients the first session is used to tell their story. This often occurs with a lack of emotional attachment to the content of their disclosure. We would expect this attachment to occur later in the relationship.

For those working with survivors of sexual trauma in a non-clinical setting an atmosphere of safety, security and containment must be achieved. Later in this chapter we will examine the practical implications of this. It is essential to carry this knowledge in ways which are not so orientated towards the strictly pragmatic. The person supporting the survivor of sexual abuse must feel able to be safe, secure and containing within him or herself. Once this point is reached the supporter will be better equipped to bear to hear the unbearable. Practical considerations around the location of meetings and communicating a sense of confidentiality will help support this. It will be communicated more importantly in many unconscious ways, all of which will be acknowledged and internalised by the survivor. The way in which, for example, a person sits or maintains eye contact while hearing about an experience of extreme trauma will tell the survivor far more about their supporter's emotional containment than any verbal communications.

Punctuality

The time spent by a client in psychotherapy is precious and should be guarded securely. Respond operates a tightly structured appointment system which places the maximum respect on the client's 50 minutes with his or her therapist by ensuring commencement and ending times are never altered, regardless of how late a client may be. This may be struggled with by some professionals who feel that if a client is unavoidably late then extra time should be allotted to the end of their session. Our belief lies in the maintenance of strict time boundaries which afford the clinical session an extra validity.

Termination of sessions

At least 24 hours' notice is required for the cancellation of a session. Respond has extensive experience of individual members of staff who will, for example, state that they believe a client's attendance at an ice-skating lesson or shopping expedition is more important than the client's clinical appointment. This provides clients with a strong message of negation of their therapeutic rights and will further invalidate their right to recovery and healing from trauma. We exist in a society whose negative perceptions surrounding psychotherapy and counselling are pervasive. It is part of the duty of a staff team to ensure they do not amplify these negative messages to their clients.

Escort duties

Clients cope better with psychotherapy when they are accompanied to the sessions by an allocated member of staff. This consistency ensures that continuity extends not only to the time spent inside the therapy session but also to the time spent outside it. We demand that members of staff remain within Respond premises while the client's session is continuing. The case of 'Phil', a middle-aged man with Down's syndrome who had experienced sexual abuse from both his parents, demonstrated the need for vigilance on this point. During one session Phil's anger at his parents overflowed and became directed at the therapist. He began to throw objects at the therapist and threatened to stab him. Phil's distress became so pronounced that he decided to end the session. On leaving the consulting room it was discovered that his escort had left Respond premises to do some shopping. The 30-minute wait for him to return was an agonising one for Phil in which his overflowing anger became focused on other clients in the waiting area, and ultimately toward himself. Fortunately other members of Respond staff were available to help support Phil in his distress. We cannot overstate the need for a consistent, reliable and sensitive escort who is able to bear the wide range of emotional responses which will be evoked by engagement in the therapeutic process.

Confidentiality

When working with a survivor of sexual abuse an agreement on confidentiality must be made explicit. We believe it to be unethical to promise pure confidentiality, as this precludes those occasions in which clients may disclose being currently abused, or may disclose having abused someone themselves. A useful introductory phrase for situations such as these is: 'Let's agree to make sure all that we talk about is kept private, unless you tell me about being hurt, or about hurting someone else.' There is a need to remind some clients of confidentiality policies. The presence of some form of confidentiality should be viewed as being part of the therapeutic process, according respect and value to the story being painfully told.

Therapeutic space

There are occasions when part of the introductory session necessitates the presence of a secure attachment figure for the client, a key worker, relative or friend who can provide tangible emotional support in a situation which for most people is characterised by fear, confusion and isolation. It is important that this remains as the exception rather than the rule. Once the client has begun to engage in the therapeutic process there may be temptations to include other members of staff within sessions in which extreme trauma is being accessed and communicated in aggressive and threatening ways. We need to be clear of the dangers inherent in any dilution of the therapeutic alliance through the inclusion of others.

Tape recording

When possible Respond tape-records all of its clinical sessions. The reasons for this are three-fold:

1. For use in clinical supervision (see below).
2. For use in any allegations of abuse made against the therapist.
3. For use in monitoring and evaluating of our clinical practices.

Care should be exercised in the recording of any clinical material. If consent is not granted by the client then recording should not occur. We recommend that a high-quality tape recorder is used to pick up the slightest sounds which may be of use within the clinical supervision setting.

Clinical supervision

All psychotherapists or counsellors working for Respond are required to receive regular clinical supervision on their caseload. Respond provides a weekly supervision group in addition to weekly individual sessions with an external psychotherapist. Audio-tape recordings of clinical sessions are transcribed and analysed either by the group or by the therapist and the clinical supervisor. In analytic terms this form of intense supervision has a great potential to uncover the unconscious processes at play within a psychotherapy session. By examining these, in conjunction with an examination of the transference and counter-transference issues at play, we are better equipped to work with the core issues described in Chapter 4.

For those members of staff engaging in therapeutic work with a survivor of sexual abuse outside the clinical setting supervision is also essential. The most highly experienced psychotherapist would be failing in her duties if she did not ensure her caseload was closely supervised. This not only provides an objective viewpoint on the clinical material, it also enables the therapist to separate her counter-transferences from the transferences evoked by the client in an attempt to uncover the underlying communications taking place.

Location

The Respond consulting rooms provide a warm, well-decorated and safe space in which clients can explore their inner worlds without undue diversions from the therapeutic task in hand. The rooms do not therefore contain telephones and remain unavailable for use by any other people while the clinical session is taking place. They contain comfortable chairs and in some cases a couch for those clients who feel secure enough not to have to maintain face-to-face contact. Each room also contains a large selection of anatomically correct dolls, small sculpture manikins, dolls houses, pens, crayons and paper. We recommend the availability of stones, rocks and pebbles with which clients may feel able to access their deeper feelings in non-verbal ways.

Panic buttons

Given the sometimes volatile nature of the issues explored within psychotherapy sessions and the disturbing effect these may have on some of our client group we recommend the placing of panic buttons inside each consultation room, group or individual. These should be connected to the rooms of members of staff who would be able to provide immediate assistance if needed. The reality is that they will be used infrequently, if at all, but may help engender a palpable air of safety and containment for clients and therapists alike.

Gender issues

Respond ensures that the wishes of clients as to the gender of their therapist are respected. To enable this to take place we have developed a team with an equal gender split. Instances of clients' wishes as to the gender of their psychotherapist being over-ridden occur more in our work with perpetrators of sexual abuse. These decisions are made through examining the forensic information available on the perpetrator and making a judgement on the appropriateness of male/female, male/male or female/female work. We would certainly steer clear of any prescriptive formula for allocation of therapists in terms of gender, as each case is unique.

Personal psychotherapy

It is a stipulated requirement that all psychotherapists and counsellors working for Respond are in personal psychotherapy. It is unrealistic to expect that working at the deep level at which we do will not have far-reaching emotional consequences on the lives of us all. Some of these may be separated within the clinical supervision setting. Most are more appropriate to work through within a personal psychotherapy space. We require this to be weekly. We would regard it as imperative that any worker struggling with the traumatic issues of disability and abuse be offered a confidential forum outside of the work setting in which to explore the powerful effects of this work upon the psyche. It appears to be particularly true of services for people with learning disabilities that emotional support for the workers is flawed or non-existent. Managerial responsibility extends to ensuring emotional support is provided. Its absence will result in staff burn out, exhaustion and ultimately loss, all of which conspire to traumatise the client group further.

Team support

The effect upon a team of working with a client with learning disabilities who has been sexually abused will be far reaching in its practical and emotional effects. Every person the client enlists throughout the telling of his or her story will have a different emotional response to hearing this story. From the person who first suspects abuse has occurred, who bears to hear the initial disclosure, who instigates an investigation, who fights for justice on behalf of the client, or remains there as confidante, enabler and advocate. Some of these roles will be separated. Often they are played by the same person.

We have seen from our work on disclosure that often the person being disclosed to is not the trained social worker or the experienced psychotherapist. It will be the trusted cook in a day centre, or the driver of the minibus. The ability of these people to bear to hear a painful story carries with it a responsibility to receive support for the effect upon them of hearing the story. This responsibility may be borne by managerial support structures, other professionals or family and friends. We have found that in many cases the support is non-existent.

In the absence of or in combination with clinical supervision members of a team supporting a victim of sexual abuse must have access to regular emotional support. In common with the support offered to the victim of sexual abuse, this support should be regular, confidential and long term. Any denial of the traumatic effects of working with survivors of sexual abuse must be acknowledged and addressed. We are all used to developing the 'martyr mentality' in this field of work – the ability to deal with the most extreme pain and anguish of our clients without ever acknowledging the presence of any of our own anguish and pain.

Training

Few of us imagined that in choosing to work with people with learning disabilities we would find ourselves working with the issues of sexual abuse and trauma. Often personal support is not enough to prevent one from feeling overwhelmed by the impact of this work, and training is called for. In terms of psychotherapy training, we have found few training bodies which are actively willing to include components on working with learning disability and sexual abuse within their training. It will be a slow and painful battle for the wider psychotherapeutic community to take on board the fact that a person with a learning disability has an equal right to psychotherapy and counselling as a person without a learning disability.

In the meantime those who find themselves working with survivors of abuse must avail themselves of the more specific training available from organisations such as Respond and NAPSAC.

Managerial accountability

The experience of being sexually abused is an isolating and stigmatising one. So too can be the experience of being disclosed to. The fact that it is more likely to be those on the lower levels of the management structure of a day centre, school or residential setting who are disclosed to necessitates strong managerial responses. We recommend the ARC/NAPSAC (1993) publication *It Could Never Happen Here* for the clarity with which it outlines structural service guidelines for the management of a disclosure of sexual abuse. This clarity should not be lost throughout the ensuing search for legal or therapeutic justice.

Policy

Once again the ARC/NAPSAC (1993) publication *It Could Never Happen Here* provides an excellent framework for any policy making procedures on the disclosure of sexual abuse by a client with learning disabilities. We recommend that all policies stress the need for ongoing therapeutic support after disclosure. Specified allocated professionals must be given responsibility for the management of this in terms of procurement and funding of therapeutic services.

Length of work

Although short-term focused counselling has been seen to have been beneficial for a limited number of clients when addressing specific issues, Respond's view underlines the need for any therapeutic work to be long term. The issues we are working with are complex, emotive and far reaching in their effects on our clients. An average length of time for our clients to remain in psychotherapy is 3 years, although some clients have continued beyond this point. An average of 44 weekly sessions take place within a year. With particularly traumatised clients (including those whose dissociation from their trauma has resulted in issues such as multiple personality disorder) the option of twice weekly psychotherapy is offered. There is a need for this to be consistent, regular and stable to enable our clients to begin to engage in a secure therapeutic attachment.

Dual diagnosis

Professionals working with survivors of sexual abuse may find themselves in a state of confusion as to the diagnosis of disability presented by their client. Many of our clients come with a dual diagnosis of mental health issues, schizophrenia or any one of a number of syndromes which may be viewed as separate from or entrenched in the diagnosis of learning disability. A psychotherapist or, indeed, any supporter of a survivor of sexual abuse, must feel equipped to utilise external consultation when necessary. Respond engages the support of consultants based in psychology and psychiatry to provide additional advice where issues of mental health, medication or suicidal impulses occur. Many of these are capable of being addressed within the confines of psychotherapy, and may clearly be viewed as manifestations of responses to trauma.

Difficulties during treatment

Counselling and psychotherapy is a healing process. The route to healing is a difficult and perilous one and it is inevitable that an exploration of any of the core issues will result in many challenging behaviours appearing to worsen. Clients accessing long-repressed feelings of rage and anger will switch suddenly from their previously passive and compliant personas to rage-filled, furious individuals. It is recommended that staff having to support such a client are made aware from the commencement of therapy of the possibility of this occurring. A useful model to share with such professionals is the mourning cycle (as outlined in Chapter 5); a process which places such externalising behaviours in the context of internalised reactions to loss. Staff will need additional support with those clients whose closer connection with their underlying emotions result in states of dissociation and multiplicity.

Funding implications

It is rare to access any form of therapeutic support which does not have funding implications, whether for the therapy itself, or for the escorting and transporting of the client to and from therapy. We advise that an allocated professional (such as a Care Manager) take responsibility for handling this aspect of the support of a survivor of sexual abuse. There will be occasions when there appears to be a dichotomy between the inner world being explored by the client and the outer world in which they are required to function. In attaining funding for any therapeutic support, the need for it to be long term must be borne in mind. If not, the very real possibility exists of the psychotherapy being curtailed due to elements beyond the client's control. Our advice is always to spell out to funders the very real implications of the premature curtailment of any therapeutic work. The mourning process has a beginning and an end. The time between the two will vary from client to client. Any attempts to induce an artificial end to a process which has not been fully experienced will re-traumatise a client, evoking memories of earlier broken attachments and losses, including the loss engendered by the experience of abuse itself.

Evaluation of psychotherapy and counselling

This area is always a contentious one in which we must consider the dilemmas surrounding client confidentiality set against the need to examine our clinical practices with an objective rigour. Clinical supervision will go some way towards ensuring that any therapeutic input, whether from an external therapeutic provider or being conducted by a layman, conforms to set standards. Respond adheres closely to the Code of Ethics laid down by the British Association of Counselling and recommends these as a useful reference point for such issues as confidentiality, ethical treatment of clients and considerations of boundaries between therapist and client. Anyone conducting work with a client who has experienced sexual abuse must be clear about their need to adopt ethical standards in how they relate to that client, how they respond to the traumatic information they are being given, and what their course of action is once a client discloses abuse that is ongoing.

Our stance on the disclosure of ongoing abuse is unequivocal. If we are told that someone is being currently sexually abused we will inform those professionals or carers who are in the best position to prevent it from continuing. This stance remains consistent whether we are working with survivors or perpetrators of sexual abuse.

Respond also employs a Research Psychotherapist to evaluate and monitor the substantial set of audio-recordings of clinical sessions we have amassed. The aim of this monitoring and evaluation is to ensure consistency of therapeutic approach and to measure in a qualitative manner the progress made by clients through their therapeutic work in terms of ability to recover from trauma, attainment of a higher level of self-esteem and increase in functioning abilities. We have a unique opportunity to reach important conclusions as to the validity of therapeutic work with a client group for whom psychotherapy and counselling have so often been denied.

Workers' wish to end

There will be times when the awful nature of the work we are engaged in will leave us feeling violated, unclean and traumatised. Many of these responses will be taken either into the clinical supervision space or the personal psychotherapy space. In some instances these spaces may never be enough and a decision will have to be reached as to the advisability of the work continuing. The option to end should not be viewed as a personal failure, for then the option is shrouded in the negative and becomes the taboo option which must never be exercised. This can only lead to greater frustration, angst and ultimate inability to carry out our responsibilities.

However, what is essential is the need for the work to be continued by someone else, and for the transition period between both workers to be managed very delicately. One of the themes of this book has been the acknowledgement of loss, a loss which becomes re-evoked most painfully with any change in staffing, or loss of secure attachment figures. The ability of our clients to deal with loss will improve throughout their time in therapy as long as any losses contained therein are acknowledged fully. This extends to losses which may appear to us to be minor but which to our clients will assume the terrible dimensions of earlier losses and abuses. Any cancellations or breaks in sessions will be difficult for clients, whose reaction may be to be overwhelmed by rejection and depression, or who may find their inner rage ignited and feel unable to demonstrate this verbally or physically. Both reactions are entirely valid, and both should be set against the context of a wider set of losses in the clients' lives.

In closing this chapter we would ask you to consider the wider professional issues which are thrown up by the issues of sexual abuse in the lives of people with learning disabilities. Sexual abuse exists against a backdrop of other abuses. These abuse are cultural, societal, everyday abuses which become so widespread that they appear to be non-abusive even to those enacting them. Every-day violations of privacy, lack of acknowledgement of sexual rights or needs and a failure to provide adequate sex education all combine to produce an abusive backdrop to the more specific sexual abuses with which we work every day. Only when the more global cultural abuses are addressed will we feel more confident about addressing the resultant instances of sexual abuse which continue to blight the lives of this vulnerable population.

References

Ainsworth, Mo, et al. (1978) *Patterns of Attachment; Assessed in the strange situation and at Home.* New Jersey; Hillsdale.

ARC and NAPSAC (1993) *It Could Never Happen Here.* London: ARC and NAPSAC Books.

Bowlby, J. (1969) *Mourning, Attachment and Loss.* Vols 1, 2, 3. London: Hogarth Press.

Bowlby, 3. (1980) *Attachment and Loss. vol. 3. Loss: Sadness and Depression.* London: Hogarth Press.

Brown, H. and Turk, V. (1993) 'The sexual abuse of adults with learning disabilities: Results of a two year incidence survey', *Mental Handicap Research,* **6**, 3.

Brown, Ho, Stein, J. and Turk, V. (1994) *Mental Handicap Research.*

Butler-Sloss, Right Honourable Lord, E. (1988) *Report of the Enquiry into Child Abuse in Cleveland, 1987.* London: HMSO.

Holmes, J. (1993) *Freud and His Father.* New York: Norton.

Kruil, M. (1986) *The Extent and Nature of Organised and Ritual Abuse.* London: HMSO.

Law Commission Report (March 1995) No 231. *Mental Incapacity.*

Mason, J.M. (1984) *The Assault on the Truth,* New York: Farrastray & Giroux.

Messler-Davies, J. and Frawley, M.G. (1994) *Treating the Adult Survivor of Childhood Sexual Abuse. A Psychoanalytic Perspective.* New York: Basic Books.

Miller, A. (1985) *The Drama of Being a Child.* London: Virago Press.

Miller, A. (1985) *For Your Own Good.* London: Virago Press.

Miller, A. (1985) *Breaking Down the Walls of Silence.* London: Virago Press.

Piantelli, A. (1992) *From Foetus To Child.* London: Routledge.

Robertson, S. (1992) A 2-year old Goes to Hospital. (film.)

SCOSAC (1991) *Assessing Suspicion* (leaflet). London: Standing Committee on Sexual Abuse of Children.

Sinason, V. (1989) 'Uncovering and responding to sexual abuse in psychotherapeutic settings'. In Brown, H. and Craft, A. (eds) *Thinking The Unthinkable – Papers on Sexual Abuse and People with Learning Difficulties.* London: FPA Education Unit.

Sinason, V. (1992) *Mental Handicap and the Human Condition.* London: Free Association Books.

Sobsey, R. (1994) *Violence and Abuse in the Lives of People With Disabilities.* Brookes.

Southgate, J. (1989) 'An introduction to the golden rules', *Journal of the Institute for Self-Analysis,* **3**(1), 13–16.

Southgate, J. (1989) 'The hidden child within us', *Journal of the Institute for Self-Analysis,* **3**(1), 4–10.

Stern, D. (1985) *The Intrapersonal World of the Infant.* New York: Basic Books.

Tate, T. (1991) *'Children for the Devil'. Ritual Abuse and Satanic Crime.* London: Methuen.

Index